PUBLIC AND
ACADEMIC HISTORY:
A Philosophy and Paradigm

PUBLIC AND ACADEMIC HISTORY:
A Philosophy and Paradigm

Phyllis K. Leffler and Joseph Brent

ROBERT E. KRIEGER PUBLISHING COMPANY
MALABAR, FLORIDA
1990

Original Edition 1990

Printed and Published by
ROBERT E. KRIEGER PUBLISHING CO., INC.
KRIEGER DRIVE
MALABAR, FLORIDA 32950

Library of Congress Cataloging-in-Publication Data

Leffler, Phyllis K.
    Public and academic history: A Philosophy and Paradigm by Phyllis K.
    Leffler and Joseph Brent
        p.   cm. —(Public history series)
    Bibliography: p.
    ISBN 0–89464–298–7 (alk. paper).—ISBN 0–89464–299–5 (pbk. :
alk. paper)
    1. Public history. 2. Historiography. I. Brent, Joseph.
    II. Title. III. Series.
    D16.163.L44 1989
    907.2—dc20   89–2628
                                                                          CIP

10 9 8 7 6 5 4 3 2

TABLE OF CONTENTS

PREFACE

In the course of writing any book, there are many people to be thanked and many explanations to be made. Any conceptual endeavor emerges out of the integration of many ideas, some of which are more our own than others. Any work of joint authorship incorporates, as well, the thoughts, skills and experiences of each of its contributors, which we choose to explain.

This endeavor emerged out of the Institute on Teaching Public History, held at Arizona State University during the summer of 1984. We found ourselves questioning some of the assumptions inherent in the Institute (see Introduction), and we searched for means to resolve those areas of discomfort. First, then, we wish to thank the directors of the Institute for offering the provocation which has resulted in this work. Wesley Johnson, Noel Stowe, Patricia Melvin Mooney, and Michael Scardaville were open to our questions, willing and eager to listen to our ideas and receptive to alternative approaches. They provided the initial catalyst for developing this new formulation. Secondly, some of the participants in the Institute, especially Cullom Davis and Ann Kaplan, took time out from a very hectic schedule to explore the ramifications of our ideas. Their support has been important to us.

In many ways, this work is an outgrowth of our respective paths as historians, and there are people who, along the path, had some role to play in its development.

v

I have spent years studying French historiography during the seventeenth and eighteenth centuries, and my understanding of historical philosophy and methodology dates from my work with John Rule while I was still a graduate student at Ohio State University. He has been a devoted friend and colleague ever since, supportive of my intellectual growth and interests. I owe him a deep debt of gratitude.

Secondly, in my teaching experiences, I have had the good fortune to work with nontraditional college students. These include the adults who ardently struggled with family and work responsibilities, but who desperately wanted their education, at The University of Tennessee at Nashville. For many of them, education was a very practical affair, and its meaning centered on the possibilities for application. In many ways, it was this constituency which made me appreciate the value of applied learning. At Tennessee State University, where I taught from 1979–1985, I encountered another teaching situation in which abstract history seemed to have little direct appeal. An able and far-sighted chairman, Bobby Lovett, recognized the desirability of incorporating a concentration in Public History, and it was this stimulus that led me to pursue the Institute sponsored by the N.E.H. I appreciate his energy and his foresight, and wish to thank him for encouraging my development in this area. Several colleagues at Tennessee State have offered both the hand of friendship and a critical reading of some of the initial stages of this manuscript. I am especially grateful to Samuel Shannon, a local and oral historian, for his continuing interest in the subject and for his thoughtful suggestions.

At the most fundamental level, however, are those who have had the deepest influence on my development. My parents, Vincent and Ann Koran, provided the discipline and support that made me believe in the value of perseverance. I am very pleased that they can finally see this work come to fruition, and am appreciative of the constant support they have shown.

Finally, and most importantly, I wish to thank my husband, Mel, who happily remained at home with our two very young children while I escaped to the Institute, and who has been not only a willing partner while this book was being written, but a source of active encouragement and support. It is his belief in the value of intellectual endeavor and in the necessity of hard work that has sustained my efforts over the past few years. More significant, it is his commitment to my personal growth, despite the temporary setbacks to his own work, that has made this possible. It is a work that owes more to him than he can ever realize.

Phyllis K. Leffler

* * * * *

I have spent thirty years studying the history of Western science and the philosophy of science, history, and the social sciences, the subjects which constitute the background and basis for this book. Two philosophers, Len Krimerman and Jim Leach, acted as guides to the fields as they were in the Sixties and introduced me to the works of Carl Hempel, Richard Rudner, H. L. A. Hart, William Dray, J. W. N. Watkins and many others. Thomas Kuhn moved my thinking in a direction which allowed me to understand the revolutionary significance of the work of Ilya Prigogine on dissipative structures when, by chance, I discovered *Order out of Chaos* in 1984. I am grateful for the knowing and challenging work of numerous contemporary writers, both academics and worldly philosophers, for helping me grasp what has been happening to the marvelous world of inquiry. Among those who come to mind as especially skillful at doing so are Paul

Davies, Benoit Mandelbrot, Heinz Pagels, Stephen Hawking, Ivar Ekeland, Gerald Feinberg, James Gleick, Ian Stewart, David Bohm, Edward Harrison, J. E. Lovelock, Abraham Pais, Gregoire Nicolis, Joseph Ford, Richard Feynman, David Berlinski and Donald J. Wilcox. They all know that by inquiring into its nature we are, as Freeman Dyson put it, "disturbing the universe."

The obvious interest among the many older black students at the University of the District of Columbia in the practical possibilities inherent in public history—as well as in its fascination for them—led me to pursue the development of the field as a genuine discipline for them and others with a similar perspective. I am grateful for the encouragement given me over several years by my friend, the public historian David Trask, in pursuing this goal.

My wife, Ann, and our grown sons, Duncan, David, and William, have each, in their distinctive ways, forcefully confirmed my intent to finish my part in this joint enterprise. I am glad they did and gratefully give them thanks.

Joseph Brent

INTRODUCTION

The idea for this book came from our intense dialogue with each other and the other participants, both students and faculty, in the Institute on Teaching Public History which met during the summer of 1984 at Arizona State University (ASU). The Institute, hosted by the ASU Graduate Program in Public History and jointly sponsored by the National Endowment for the Humanities and the National Council on Public History, had the unintended effect of raising fundamental questions about the discipline of history itself, even though its major focus was the much narrower and utilitarian goal of teaching us how to "do" public history.

The assumption which underlay the Institute was that historians needed training to teach "public" history because it somehow constituted a different or at least distinctive type of historical inquiry. A second assumption was that those who *used* history in the public arena were involved in a "profession" far different from those who taught history in an academic setting. In either case, the implicit message of the Institute was that there was an inevitable separation between "traditional" history programs which focused on academic texts and more innovative public history programs which were oriented toward activity and public promotion of history.

We believe that this unfortunate division between those who view themselves as academic historians and those who see themselves as public historians can be resolved only by

1

inquiring into the nature of history as a discipline. This, in turn, will lead us to reexamine the long-standing arguments about historical methodology and about the position of history along the continuum of knowledge. In the process, we will be discussing some fundamental changes in the nature of science, which make the century-long quarrel between the sciences and the humanities no longer real, and which also make it possible for history to be once more a discipline central to understanding.

History, in whatever guise, has always been the most important way any people, no matter how small their numbers, understood who they were, are, and might become. As societies became more complex, so did their histories, moving from expanded genealogies to intricate and often mythic and elaborate crystallizations of the events of thousands of years. These historical constructs began to include so many social elements that they eventually came to characterize whole regions of the globe—Greece, Rome, Christendom, Islam, the West. Differences were regarded as internal to these great categories, so that even when large-scale events threatened or actually undermined their unity, the sense of historical identity remained unimpaired. Indeed, "the West," for example, seemed to perceive itself as able to engulf whatever culture was different from it, even as its elements appeared intent on destroying each other.

By the late nineteenth century, however, worldwide commerce of great diversity, immensely more powerful technology, and industrialization produced internal changes which had the effect of breaking up the unity of these large historic identities and replacing them with myriad new ways of doing things: with methods, especially the methods of science. For history, as we will show, the attempt to create a scientifically validated discipline not only fragmented the way history was done, but fractured the larger sense of unity as well and separated written history from its traditional audiences. The reappearance over the past two decades of a more publicly oriented history, in addition to providing trained historians with much needed jobs, makes it possible for the discipline to reenter the world of affairs and to participate directly in the construction of new historical syntheses to account for and give meaning to the great and profoundly unsettling changes which transform our world.[1]

What we propose in this book is nothing less than the reconciliation of academic and public history by means of their common methodology. We show both how they became separate and how they can be rejoined to produce what we believe to be a unified discipline better, though more difficult, than either one practiced separately.

We begin with an analysis of history and its audiences. The first chapter describes the current crisis within the discipline, examines the present divisions between the "public" and "academic" markets for history, the nature of existing public history programs, the failures which have resulted from the devaluation of history and the ethical problems arising from the practice of public history.

The second chapter addresses the argument over the values of scientific and humane learning and knowledge as they affect the discipline of history. We propose that it is no longer possible to accept the broadly unquestioned claim of nineteenth and early twentieth century science that science alone can produce objective and predictive knowledge of the world. Developments in science itself have brought the Newtonian synthesis into such question that it can no longer stand. We suggest that the century-long attempt by historians to create a scientific discipline of history, largely by copying the social sciences, has been mistaken and has tended to undermine those elements of knowledge which are essentially historical.

In our third chapter, we develop a model, using the works of the historian, Fernand Braudel, and the Nobel-laureate chemist, Ilya Prigogine, which demonstrates the probability that a common method is used for all human inquiry, whether or not it is termed "scientific." We show how the attack on the possibility of objectivity originated in physics and has direct application for history (and by implication for any discipline) and we explain the utility of this model for the training of historians, both "academic" and "public." This chapter ends by relating epistemology and methodology to process. We establish a paradigm for teaching history based on the fundamental historical processes of research, analysis, and presentation. We propose, in short, a variable program design for the teaching of both public and academic history.

The program design has been tested in four different academic settings. Courses were offered in three distinct areas to students of very diverse backgrounds. Each time the model was offered it was modified to suit the student and course needs. In one case, a course was offered as a lecture/ discussion class for both graduate and undergraduate students without prerequisites; in another, a course was structured as a writing seminar for senior history majors; in another, the model was used as a basis for a tutorial; and in yet another, the model was used as an integral part of a course for senior students in another field.

Each of the institutions in which this program design was tested offered a different kind of student body. Tennessee State University (TSU) and the University of the District of Columbia (UDC) are both historically black institutions with a significant adult student population, but the second is distinctively more urban and diverse, with a large proportion of foreign born students from Africa, Central America and Southeast Asia. The University of Virginia (UVA) serves a predominantly white and traditional student body.

Moreover, the places where these courses were offered are themselves significant in their differences. Nashville is a medium-sized city well aware of its regional history. Its historical resources date from the late eighteenth century and include historic buildings, a state-supported history museum, a state library and archives, private universities (including Vanderbilt and Fisk), several major editing projects, and the celebrated country music industry. The city is also the headquarters for the American Association of State and Local History, an agency deeply involved in promoting the American past through workshops and seminars for history's practitioners and for those who preserve the material cultural heritage of this nation. While Nashville is a center for provincial culture, the diversity of its resources provides a rich basis of support for the program we outline.

Washington, D.C., of course, is filled with public agencies whose history is central to understanding the national past. It is home to major museums and archives, both public and private. The national agencies and private associations which abound in the city are all involved in policy making, often at the national level and their past and perspectives provide the sources for a hundred useful projects. The city itself has its own local history from which much can be learned about the development of social patterns. Obviously, the city's resources offer an almost unlimited basis for doing public history.

Charlottesville, on the other hand, is a very small and unique city—less than one-tenth the size of Nashville and a smaller fraction the size of Washington. Despite its size, it is famous for its early history and its heroes, three of whose homes (Jefferson, Madison, and Monroe) are located in the surrounding countryside. The University of Virginia, Jefferson's "academical village," remains as artifactual evidence of his educational values. This ambience, editing projects on

the papers of Washington and Madison, a university program in historical architecture, the Albemarle County Historical Society, and other resources make Charlottesville a
specialized and narrow, but deep-reaching basis for the study
of public history.

The validity of our program design has been shown by
the success of trial courses in all three environments. We
had no difficulty in involving those outside the academy in
helping us to transmit their enthusiasm for the world of
history beyond the covers of books. They willingly and ea-
gerly volunteered their time and knowledge for the cause of
public history. The students, representing a wide spectrum
of abilities and experiences, uniformly found that our
courses provided significant excitements of history. For
many of them, even those who were history majors, they
understood for the first time the reasons which lay behind
their interest.

Two hypothetical examples may suffice to illustrate the
kinds of possibilities which our approach to history as a unified discipline makes possible to improve the traditional history curriculum for students. A course given in a major
urban area on the subject of ancient Greece or Rome would
require that students study museum exhibits and artifacts
from the period and place. Such study would bring students
to understand aesthetic, economic, intellectual, and social
dimensions not available from their readings. They would
learn, in the words of Simon Bronner, that

> Material culture is made up of tangible things crafted, shaped, al-
> tered, and used across time and across space. It is inherently per-
> sonal and social, mental and physical. It is art, architecture, food,
> clothing, and furnishing. But more so, it is the weave of these objects
> in the everyday lives of individuals and communities. It is the mi-
> gration and settlement, custom and practice, production and con-
> sumption that is . . . history and culture. It is the gestures and

processes that extend ideas and feelings into three-dimensional form.[2]

Asked to evaluate the effectiveness of the assigned museum exhibit, the students would increase their familiarity with the research potential of material culture and would also develop an appreciation of the challenges involved in such research for the interpretation of the past and the presentation of their results.

Or consider a survey of recent United States history in which students are required to explore the written, artifactual, and oral remains of the past in the local community. While such an approach may appear unnecessarily complicated at first glance, reflection on the nature of the community from which the students come will reveal how useful such a way of proceeding can be. The following questions should be suggestive: When and under what circumstances was the community founded? What are the written, artifactual, and oral evidences that reveal its history? What larger national events affected its existence—immigration, migration, industrialization? What characteristics remain which reveal its history? What parts of its history are lost in one kind of evidence that can be reconstructed from the other two kinds?

By exploring questions such as these in the context of the more general traditional academic course, students will be able to comprehend the importance and relevance of issues and questions which are often merely abstract for them. They will understand the significance of history in their own environment, which is necessarily the first step to more general historical understanding. They will appreciate the interdependence of academic learning and daily life. They will come to understand the links between the particular and the general. They will perceive, usually for the first time, that connections do exist between individual experience, trends and patterns, and the almost unchanging bases of human life.

For students intending to enter the world of affairs with training in public history, the program suggested here will introduce both the academic and practical knowledge necessary for their professional competence.

In short, then, this book bridges the existing breach between the worlds of public and academic history by providing the philosophical underpinning for a novel teaching methodology. For specific application of this methodology, a companion volume, entitled *Public History: A Book of Readings* is also published. Through an anthology of readings, we illustrate how the model and method herein described can be applied. By focusing on historical perspectives and processes in the context of both public and academic history, we provide in the companion volume the concrete mechanism for reunification of the profession of history. This second volume is intended to be used in conjunction with the philosophy and paradigm presented here. Its components, focusing on the conceptualization of time and order and on the processes of historical inquiry, expand upon the historical methodology proposed in Chapter 3 of this book. Taken together, this work and the companion volume illustrate how the discipline of history is enriched by the integration of its public and academic contexts.

NOTES

1. William H. McNeill, *Mythhistory and Other Essays* (Chicago: University of Chicago Press, 1986), 3–42.
2. Simon Bronner, "The Idea of the Folk Artifact," in *American Culture and Folklife* (Ann Arbor: University of Michigan Research Press, 1985), 3.

Chapter 1

HISTORY AND ITS AUDIENCES

In the United States, history, both as discipline and subject, has fallen on hard times. The most noticeable sign of this depressed state is the deep public ignorance of the essential facts of the national past. The discipline is too often reduced to isolated, technical conversations among its academic practitioners. The subject has lost its power to provide understanding of past events to the general public and its leaders. In part, these conditions are a natural consequence of a culture which no longer agrees on a valued, common tradition to which anyone can refer and be understood. In part, they are the consequence of the impact of the scientific method on all disciplines over the past century with its tendency to reduce events to their simplest elements while simultaneously bringing general syntheses into question. Ethnic, religious and economic groups, the sexes, the generations, and the regions cannot agree upon the bare essentials of how the present became what it is. At the same time, researches into the past are increasingly concerned with narrow, clearly limited issues of little general interest or significance, even to academic historians. It is hardly surprising, then, that history would lose its status as a necessary basis of human knowledge.

But for history to lose its once high status in the hierarchy of disciplines is not to lose its necessity for the acquisition of any kind of knowledge. Memory, no matter how we may choose to define it, is essential for every operation of the mind. Without it, we could not perceive a series, we could not count or narrate. If memory were in some way seriously impaired, and we could not remember things except for a short time, most operations necessary to our survival as a species would be endangered. If our memory in all its aspects, especially those of which we are least aware, should be completely destroyed, we would all face immediate cultural death. There would be no language for communicating or thinking, no activity, no learning, no short or long, no duration, no expanse, no transition, no motion. Continuity and beginnings would have no existence for us. Since all human society is made up of individuals, to the extent that our common memory is impaired, to that extent our ability to act effectively in common is equally defective. The loss of a society's memory is no different in the depth of its effect on the collective than is amnesia on the individual, because the collective memory—history as it is known—exists in individual minds.

In times before the complexities introduced by industrialization and modern technology, history's role was simpler. Thucydides, the exiled Athenian admiral writing 2500 years ago about the historical meaning of the great wars of his time, wrote only for members of his small, elite and literate class—who shared completely the same cultural baggage. The rest of Greek society was so little noticed that what scant evidence of it that exists comes from the point of view of that elite.

At another extreme, represented by the early portions of the Old Testament or any other example of an oral tradition handed down by rote from generation to generation, all the members of a tribe knew the same history by word of mouth and could refer to it easily for the resolution of most disputes and problems. In these two cases and all others like them, history's audiences were culturally homogenous and so did not find themselves in disputes about what was basic to their worlds. Instead, they argued about the meanings of these essentials.

Before the late nineteenth century, whether they were literate or not, historians were not members of an academic discipline called History. Thucydides, or in later Roman times, Julius Caesar, a general who became emperor, were scholarly men of affairs who wrote history as advocates of a point of view. The same can be said of the premodern historians of China and Islam. In medieval Europe, history was written by churchmen or those educated in the church. In Europe, with the decline of church authority by the eighteenth century, history, though increasingly thought of as a subject of its own, was again a serious pastime of scholarly men of affairs like the Englishman, Edward Gibbon, whose monumental *Decline and Fall of the Roman Empire* was researched, written and published during the period of the American Revolution at the same time he served in Parliament and on the Board of Trade. Gibbon believed that the peak of civilization was Rome's Augustan Age.

It was at the end of the nineteenth century that history in the West, largely under the influence of German scholars claiming scientific credentials, became an independent academic discipline to which entry was gained only through the possession of advanced degrees. With this change, history increasingly became perceived as a disinterested, scientific, objective and academic enterprise, intrinsically much more valuable than the untrained and partisan productions of men of affairs, no matter how scholarly.

By the 1960s, academic historians steadily moved away from general and synthetic historical studies often presented in multivolume formats toward specialized and analytic studies. This movement was accompanied by a gradual but drastic change in the audiences for which historians wrote. Historical study and meaning were no longer embedded in the public process and a reflection of it, but isolated in the academy. The presumption was, and in many cases is, that this isolation brought with it objectivity, as if academic historians somehow were more able to escape from their culture by earning an advanced degree than were their less educated fellows.

With the steady shift from privileged to general education in the colleges and universities which began at the end of World War II and intensified in the fifties and sixties, the history taught at every level of education proved increasingly unpalatable to students who then took their dislike with them into public life. Most of these students found the standard interpretations of the past quite at variance with their own experience and often demeaning to it. The general reading public had long before dropped academic historians in favor of popular authors and their own folk traditions.

By the 1970s, the subject of history, and consequently the profession of history, had entered a state of crisis where it still remains. Colleges and universities reported a rapidly declining interest among students, inability to tenure faculty, and often the necessity to eliminate formerly popular courses and to cut back faculty as well. On the other hand, as the isolation of academic history suggests, small, local museums have proliferated in response to popular interest, while the funds to support the activities and professionals associated with them are far below what is needed.[1] History as a field for popular amusement also continues to grow. County fairs which document the history of a local region; crafts festivals which celebrate the artifacts and skills of old-time craftsmen; historic houses which represent the lifestyles of departed aristocracies; historical films and novels which transport their viewers into imagined worlds of romance and valor; museums of "living history" which claim accurate recreation of the life of an earlier era; all these and more appeal to larger numbers of people. The impression is generated that as a society we enjoy and value history.

The reality is otherwise. The public *does* enjoy history as nostalgia, romance or genealogy. Academic historians, however, have steadily undermined the public impact of their discipline over the past half-century. Their unsuccessful attempts to make history a clearly defined discipline with a justifiable scientific basis and narrow specializations have denuded history of both its synthetic power and its diverse audiences.

Outside the academy, history has been made to appeal to a public largely ignorant of its past by means of attractively simplified vignettes of that past. A well-designed exhibit, aimed specifically at a visual audience is deemed successful for the attention it attracts, usually measured by the number of visitors. A history fair, given in an appropriate location such as a village green or city square, often becomes a social event, complete with food, balloons, games and whole families. Events of this kind, packaged and marketed for specific public groups, do bring together large numbers of people, but do not and cannot develop the sense of a shared and meaningful past. Their success is too much measured in numbers and enthusiasm and too little in terms of the creation of mutual historical understanding.

Within the academy, historians have increasingly moved to the transformation of history into a social science. The ability to use the methodologies, models, and techniques of the social sciences, whether as quantification, theory or other adaptations from anthropology, economics, sociology, psychology, and political science, have dominated advanced training in history almost to the exclusion of concern with time and human experience. Strong opposition from a significant minority of historians who consider history, along with literature, philosophy, and the arts, as a humanities has not had much of an impact. Most Ph.D. dissertations are narrowly circumscribed to conform to a scientific model of expertise. The result has been that academically trained historians speak to fewer and fewer audiences with smaller and smaller numbers. They even have trouble conversing among themselves, behaving as if history were divided into airtight compartments. The broader public is disaffected if not left out in the cold. The student audience has dropped drastically with a decline of about 60% in undergraduate B.A. degrees awarded in history between 1970 and 1982.[2]

While great disagreement exists among academic historians about the way to rectify the decline of history, two solutions are regularly put forward as workable: (1) to offer attractive courses to bring back the students and (2) to make the discipline into more and more of a social science as the means to achieve greater professional acceptance. As the undergraduate audience continues to scatter to other fields of interest in the social sciences and business, and those with new Ph.D.'s in history either find it impossible to obtain permanent, tenure-track positions, or else obtain them only to be forced out of the field anyway on the average of six years later, these alternatives do not appear effective.

Despite these ominous trends, if they turn their attention outside the academy, professionally trained historians will see that they do not face a future as bleak as it appears. Other publics exist whom a small minority of academic historians have long recognized as legitimate employers of their trained students. These external possibilities exist in spite of the refusal of a majority of academic historians to realize that the discipline is in its nature something far more than purely academic. For the minority, whose motives are often understandably a matter of employment, new and practical opportunities exist for the practice of history having little or nothing to do with the academy.

THE MACROSCOPIC AUDIENCE: THE PUBLIC

Despite its specialties and specializations, history is a subject for the convinced generalist. No subject is exempt in principle from the examination of its history, even history itself. No other discipline is concerned so intimately with the question of how the present became what it is. Because the study of history creates the public memory without which no social organization survives, it is well-educated, trained historians who bring the specific skills which help explain to the various publics what has changed over time and what that change may mean for them. Whether the audience be international or national, local or regional, institutional or informal; concerned with propaganda or truth, policy or administration; whatever that audience may be and do, it requires useful knowledge of its past. Organizations such as the International Red Cross, The World Bank, General Motors, the City of Reno, Nevada, the Roman Catholic Church, could all, along with an indefinite number of others, benefit from a close knowledge of their histories. Other organizations of many and varied sorts have already learned the benefits of employing trained historians.

Dozens of agencies of the United States Government utilize the services of those with historical training. These include the Departments of Agriculture, Commerce, Defense, Energy, Interior, Housing and Urban Development, Labor and State. Some have positions specifically named "historian"; others have Historical Offices; some simply use those with historical training, but classify their positions by other titles, such as researcher, conservator and analyst. Each has its own research divisions and planning staffs. Under the Department of the Interior fall smaller units, such as Indian Affairs, Land Management, Minerals Management, and the National Park Service—the last administering hundreds of national historic sites. The Department of State has a large historical office. Similarly, the Department of Energy employs a public historian as the head of its archival materials collection. Training in history with additional archival or library science skills has often led to employment within the General Services Administration which oversees the National Archives and Records Service, or within the Library of Congress. Skilled researchers and writers are regularly sought as staff personnel by Congress. Many national agencies engage in regular analysis of their policies and often employ historians on their staffs as does, for example, the policy and planning division of the Environmental Protection Agency. National museums need and use the skills of historians, ranging from the Smithsonian Institution to the Frederick Douglass Memorial Home and Ford's Theatre. Most historians involved in training graduate students in history fail to recognize the opportunities for employing historians outside the academy and have thereby contributed to the present crisis.

Opportunities for trained historians extend well beyond the boundaries of the federal government. Every level of state and local government uses historians to study and maintain historical records and sites, such as battlefields, homes, and artifacts of all kinds. These activities are an important aspect of the creation of the sense of local identities which abound throughout the nation.

Some cities, like Detroit, New York, and Houston, commit funds for the position of city historian. They do so for two reasons. The first is the entirely practical necessity for keeping and maintaining records important to governing because they provide, in addition to needed documentation, the basis for the continuing policy analysis and planning which underlies both legislation and administration. The second is the recognition by public officials that it is in their interest to enrich the present through the past. In a large, rambling federation like the United States, it is easy to overlook and difficult to demonstrate the great significance of local history for a collective understanding of the national past. It is to a large extent the historical committees and commissions on the state and local levels which carry out the preservation efforts, support the research designed to protect that heritage, and encourage the public's involvement with its past.

Within the sphere of private interests, there also exist substantial opportunities for trained historians which, in turn, spawn new audiences for history in a process only in its beginnings. First are those nonprofit organizations, such as research institutes, museums, historical societies, libraries, labor unions, communities, and churches. Second are small businesses, including a variety of consulting firms in community resource management, research, and policy analysis. Historians for hire, to carry out legal research, land management studies, historical impact studies, and a variety of similarly historically oriented projects, are a small but growing minority among professional historians. Third are the large corporate establishments in every field, such as manufacturing, banking, law, media and communications, marketing and distribution, a knowledge of whose histories is becoming of critical importance for effective management.

During the past two decades corporate leadership has recognized the necessity for maintaining company archives to preserve records for research and planning, for policy analysis, for public relations purposes, and to project that company identity which best serves to raise personnel morale. Such diverse corporations as General Electric, Cities Service, the Salt River Project in Phoenix, Arizona, the New York Stock Exchange, and the Los Angeles Power and Light Company maintain full-time historians for a variety of purposes. Banks are among those private institutions with a particular interest in the preservation of their histories. A leader is the

Wells Fargo Bank which maintains a large public museum to present the early history of banking in Los Angeles. Other corporations, one example being Henry Ford's museum of automotive history in Greenfield, Michigan, have also established museums to trace the history of their industry.

Museums are, in general, an expansive field which appeal to a large public, seeking diversion along the crossroads of America. Whether it be Colonial Williamsburg, Disney World, or Stockbridge Village, "Living History," in which the museum is itself an attempt to recreate a specific past location and time complete with actors and craftspersons, is an increasingly popular means of representing the past. The more historians are involved in such reenactments, the more valid, as well as entertaining, they can be expected to be.

Specific audiences for history are many and varied. They exist both as prospective employers of trained historians and as public consumers of the past. These two elements are interdependent because an increased public interest in history and its significance creates a greater demand for historians. Professional historians should, therefore, carefully consider the benefits to be derived from becoming directly involved in a public history which applies the methods and techniques of the profession to nontraditional questions and topics, often for audiences and clients who are not themselves part of the usual disciplinary circles and specializations. To advocate public history requires at the outset that programs specifically designed for its requirements be developed and taught either as a part of or in addition to the traditional curriculum in history.

THE MICROSCOPIC AUDIENCE: THE STUDENTS

Even the most cursory examination of college and university catalogs shows clearly the remarkable lack of change in the history curriculum over the past four decades. Despite extraordinary changes in society, technology, professional requirements, and cultural perspectives, departments of history have seldom moved from the traditional curriculum with its periodizations created in the late nineteenth century. Courses in Medieval, Renaissance and Reformation, Early Modern and Modern European History are still the standard, though such slices of time are often not only no longer useful but misleading as well. Survey courses in United States History still break at the Civil War, as they did fifty years ago, even though the difficult history which has occurred since then would easily overstuff two semesters. Advanced courses in Civil War and Reconstruction are still largely about issues as they were defined by historians over a century ago, even though the subject of such courses includes many more equally substantial issues arising out of more recent controversies. The same kinds of criticisms can and have been leveled at most departmental programs. In large part because of criticism, courses have been added in the subjects of economic, immigrant, social, women's and black history and, more rarely, in the history of science and technology. The addition of these courses has done little more than create a confusion of purposes. Such additions have seldom led to the creation of integrated programs in history, flexibly designed to take advantage of changes in historical perspective. Instead, the almost universal departmental strategy has been to adopt, without irony, the business approach and give the shoppers whatever they will buy.

Departments have often argued that any student taking a full program in history at any competent college or university would develop the specific historical skills required by the discipline as a matter of course. If so, because the training would be haphazard rather than programmatic, its success would depend more on the student's choice of professors— or the institution itself—than on the program of study.

Moreover, despite the freedom of choice offered undergraduate students, interest in history, both as subject and
major, continues to decline, a fact which demonstrates
clearly enough that academic programs of history are in need
of thoroughgoing reform. Even those departments in large
institutions whose enrollments are raised by the artificial
demand imposed by general requirements at the undergraduate level find it difficult to attract graduate students
and to place them effectively.

THE REEMERGENCE OF PUBLIC HISTORY

In 1976, the bicentennial year of the American Revolution, five professional historical associations, among them
the American Historical Association (AHA) and the Organization of American Historians (OAH), joined to form the
National Coordinating Committee for the Promotion of History (NCCPH). This action was the first formal recognition
of the seriousness of the discipline's decline. Its goals,
unique for including the idea of selling history, were:

> . . . to promote historical studies generally, but especially in the
> schools at all levels, to broaden historical knowledge among the
> general public, to restore confidence in the discipline of history
> throughout society and to educate employers in the public and
> private sectors to the value of employing professional historians.[3]

At the time there existed only one kind of public history,
defined by the local historical agencies and museums, which
were and are its bailiwick and is represented by the American
Association of State and Local History (AASLH). Now there
exists a second, of very recent origin—a consequence in part
of the formation of the NCCPH—which is both much
broader in scope and far more ambitious in intent. It is
represented by the National Council of Public History

(NCPH), formalized in 1980, and by its publication, *The Public Historian*, which first appeared in the fall of 1978.

The first type is very much limited by local historical interests and is, as one of its practitioners put it, "history on a shoe string"—a poverty-ridden field with most salaries below $15,000, although a few private historical associations and some state agencies pay well.[4] The second, arising as it has from two decades' steady decline of interest in academic history—in its development much like that made earlier by the social sciences—is a movement out of the academy into the "real world." It constitutes a serious attempt to professionalize the discipline and has its origins in the intent to broaden the discipline of history. In 1985, there were at least fifty operating programs nationally in history departments. These were located in public and private colleges and universities and a number of other educational and research institutions. In 1981, the majority of salaries for this type of public historian, working in seven areas (research/archive/museum, historic preservation, information management, general administration, business/complex organization, policy planning/evaluation and teaching) clustered between $15,000 and $37,500 and averaged $27,500, although a substantial number were paid $35,000 and over.[5] Public history has not yet become a highly paid career. Financial problems are particularly acute in small and local organizations.

Both groups have established close ties with academically-based historians in order to promote the expansion of the field and to maintain its quality. The National Council on Public History and the American Association of State and Local History regularly sponsor a variety of interactions between public and academic historians through conferences, journals, newsletters, and other publications. However, while these activities are supported by the American Historical Association and the Organization of American Historians, the majority of historians in colleges and universities have no knowledge or only a vague understanding of the potential for expanding the profession, or else actively oppose it.

PROGRAMS IN PUBLIC HISTORY

In 1980–81, the NCPH and the AHA sponsored a survey of the field of public history.[6] At the time, only four years after the formation of the NCCPH and in the year the NCPH was inaugurated, virtually all the 2,347 respondents were the graduates of academic programs with no public orientation. Asking professionally trained historians working outside the academy what they considered *positive* attributes of their training elicited this pattern of responses:

> "Persistence in seeking answers and/or evidence; exposure to cultural trends and backgrounds; tendency to see events and people in context."
> "They like to read books which is no longer of much value in this society."
> "I am not qualified to answer this question, not having discovered any (positive attributes) that result from a student's history education."
> "The history background has no positive attributes. Only the person has positive attributes and those are what determines a positive or negative use of his/her history background."

To this group, most academic history as taught appeared archaic, abstract, wrongheaded, and out-of-touch. At best, apparently, history offered a vague sense of perspective. Startlingly absent from these responses was any mention of specific historical skills and methodology; indeed, no concrete value was ascribed to the discipline for understanding and explaining past events.

On the other hand, negative attributes were described specifically as being of four kinds: the slower speed at which historians work compared to business practice; the academically narrow understanding of the meaning of the word, "career"; a condescension and disdain for the world of affairs; and an unwillingness or inability to engage in teamwork.

On the subject of academic history programs, the questionnaire brought forth comments such as these:

"Reduce the number of students specializing in history and cut the history programs beyond the MA by half."

"I do not encourage anyone to major in history and know of several employees in my section alone who are taking other courses to be able to leave the history field, myself included."

"I do not support encouraging people to go into history with the idea that it is a route to business employment."

"History + Graduate Trade School = Job."

"I cannot encourage others to major in history. The job market is bleak and will remain so in the foreseeable future. If I could start over again, I would do an undergraduate history course and then get an MBA or a CPA and go to work for a corporation or a stock brokerage firm. I would use history as an avocation, not as a vocation."

"This is not so much a suggestion as a question. I cannot for the life of me understand what the graduate program in public history at [the University of California at Santa Barbara] or any similar program could possibly be teaching. Are their students getting jobs? What are they learning? Pray tell! . . ."

In response to the disaffection with academic history expressed in these responses from its students, at first a few, and now a steadily increasing number of departments of history have responded radically to the decline of their discipline by introducing programs in applied or public history. These concentrate on adapting the historian's skills and methodology to existing or potential markets. It is conven-

ient to consider these programs as falling into three broad
categories.

First is the practical, businesslike approach in which students are trained to seek out potential employers or to explore policy issues in ways that cater to the needs of identifiable clients. These programs are broad-based in scope and
continue to train students as generalists. An example is the
graduate program at the University of California at Santa
Barbara which exemplifies the "historian-as-consultant"
mode. The aim is to train professional historians as private
consultants who will then be able to sell their skills to paying
clients. In a market that has proved catastrophic for academically trained historians, these public historians have had
limited but substantial success. A recent survey showed that
fifty of sixty graduates of the program were placed. Even
so, some of them complained that in the process of going
public they lost the rigorous training in the researching,
analyzing, interpreting and writing skills basic to the discipline. Perhaps to address this need for the essentials of training in history, Robert Kelley introduced in 1986 an undergraduate major in the program to study the history of public
policy. He writes:

> By studying the history of public policy, rather than simply the way
> the process seems to work right now in the present scene, students
> acquire the deep dimension of time. . . . The goal is to send people
> out into public life who have a clear sense of what they are going
> into, how it works, and what they can expect.[7]

While it is too early to measure the success of this interdisciplinary undergraduate degree, it does provide one model
for combining in the same department undergraduate and
graduate offerings in public history which are mutually consistent and supportive of both academic and public requirements.

A second type of program follows the model provided in the social sciences by adapting the discipline to meet public interests and demands. Students are trained to focus on a particular aspect of the discipline, such as archival administration, museology, publishing and editing, historic preservation, business history, or the media. Programs of this sort are now in place at Arizona State University, the University of California at Riverside, the University of Connecticut, Colorado State University, the University of Maryland, Middle Tennessee State University, and New York University. Operating at the graduate level, these programs emphasize the particular skills which will enable academic historians, now public historians, to sell their wares to libraries, museums, communities, and corporations.

Directors of such programs recognize the failure of the traditional model to prepare students for any but an academic career. At the same time, they are also well aware that history is not a discipline which translates as easily into public practice as does, for example, economics into the world of business. Applied history programs which concentrate on a specific aspect of the world of affairs must be able to train students to create a bridge between history and an enterprise such as business. Thus, Noel Stowe of Arizona State University, director of a program in business and history, insists that the curriculum enhance the special attributes of the historian's discipline while applying them to the business world:

> . . . the basic point to be stressed is the connection between history (as subject and process) and business, its problems, issues, and questions. Students will learn to use historical process to make judgments about questions . . . that must be studied from a historical perspective yet are rarely considered directly in graduate level courses.[8]

Some of these professionally oriented programs not only teach the application of historical method, but also affirm it as their responsibility to communicate a particular and self-conscious social perspective to their students. The New York University Program describes itself as one which:

> . . . provides training in the New Social History, enabling historians to reconceptualize history and reach new audiences.[9]

The New Social History, with its openly Marxist ideology, is clearly directed at programs, such as that at Arizona State University, which appear to reflect uncritically a commonly accepted capitalist perspective in their approach to business history and toward history in general. This criticism of public history is partially motivated by the desire of radical historians to claim the new arena as their own, as Howard Green makes clear in his critique of the public history movement for failing to redefine " . . . the nature of authority within the historical profession or in the society at large."[10]

The third category of public history programs exhibits an orientation toward problem solving and policy analysis. In it the curriculum and methodology of history are perceived as the means to better control events and are put forward as management tools. In the original version, the John F. Kennedy School of Government at Harvard University employs a "case-method" approach to demonstrate the practical—that is, nonspeculative—utility of historical analysis for those who govern. In their book, *Thinking in Time*, Richard Neustadt and Ernest May describe this approach, which they do not believe requires great historical learning:

> Thinking of time in such a way appears . . . to have three components. One is recognition that the future has no place to come from but the past, hence the past has predictive value. Another element is recognition that what matters for the future in the present is departures from the past, alterations, changes, which prospectively or actually divert familiar flows from accustomed channels, thus affecting that predictive value. A third component is continuous comparison, an almost constant oscillation from present to past to

future and back, heedful of prospective change, concerned to ex-
pedite, limit, guide, counter or accept it as the fruits of comparison
suggest.[11]

This kind of program in applied history for government officials and business managers has been adopted by such universities as California at Berkeley, Carnegie-Mellon, North
Carolina at Chapel Hill, and by the Rand Graduate Institute.

These three types of programs in public history, representing a return to an older emphasis, have emerged in the
intersection between the academic discipline and public life.
In summary, what public historians do is closely similar to
what historians have always done in the more familiar activities of teaching and research. They bring to the history of
an institution or other organization the same skills of the
professional generalist: the knowledge of varied techniques
of research and analysis, an ability to analyze widely diverse
data, and the capacity to express their findings cogently and
coherently. Public history, however, vastly extends the areas
in which these skills can be applied and changes the relationship between historians and clients. Despite their novelty
and limitations, these programs have had remarkably better
success in placing students in jobs related to history than
have traditional academic programs, achieving a rate of
placement estimated at 80% or better.[12]

A pioneering spirit pervades the advocates of this new
field. It is expressed in their perception of how they differ
from their colleagues in the academy. Such colleagues are
described as impractical, recondite, and inexperienced in the
very world whose past they mean to explain. Public historians
contrast the purely academic interests of the ivory tower with
their own practical concern to meet client needs and dead-
lines, to live within budgetary restraints for which they are
responsible, and to learn methodologies and skills foreign
to traditional history. They have succeeded in creating a

movement which does not see history as an end in itself or
as the means to the creation of an educated and cultured
citizen, but which instead puts forward the ideal of the
"professional historian" who understands how to balance
the requirements of the discipline with client demands and
the availability of resources for research with the demands
for working results. Public historians have trained their students to develop managerial skills, team-research methodologies and professional styles. They have taught their students problem-oriented research techniques, using
unorthodox sources and accepting constraints from their
clients. In creating this new dimension for working historians, they have also raised a serious question: does entering
the marketplace itself endanger the essential values of the
discipline?

THE ETHICS OF PROFESSIONAL HISTORY

When, in the 1870s and 1880s, the discipline of history
left public life to enter the academy, its practitioners believed
they spoke with the objective and unified voice of science.
Now, a century later, as many of them leave the academy to
reopen the interrupted dialogue with the world of affairs,
they speak in a babel of voices and languages and cannot
even agree on the essential elements of the discipline. In
these circumstances, it is difficult to inquire into what constitutes proper professional conduct for historians, because
it is not clear even to them what it is they do. One consequence of this confusion has been the issuing of a number
of different codes of ethics for different aspects of the fragmented discipline, such as archivists, oral historians, mu-
seologists, federal historians, archaeologists, the California
Committee for the Promotion of History, and the National
Council on Public History.

Another consequence has been to uncover qualities of the discipline which were not apparent in its academic guise. Particularly, as Ronald C. Tobey shows, the move by historians to reengage the world of affairs, awkward as it has been, has reestablished the truth that advocacy, though it is much denied, is an inescapable and intrinsic element of practicing of history in a public setting.[13] As sociologists might say, this value-charged nature of the discipline underlines its methodological similarity with that of the law. Thirty years ago, Hart and Honoré pointed out that law and history both necessarily involve the appraisal of value in making the causal judgments by which they explain events.[14] History, most obviously in its public setting but also in principle, is not disinterested and its practitioners are, therefore, advocates. This was always so and the century-long flirtation of academic historians with the increasingly controversial ideal of objective, or value-free, inquiry has never obscured their profound concern with the meaning of the past. Tobey observes that for a discipline of this kind,

> ... scholarship in this ... setting ... is necessarily advocative in character, and cannot prima facie be objective or disinterested. At the same time, the implicit bias of this advocacy is dealt with by rules and procedures. In other words, in the public setting, fairness in scholarship is not only substantial, but is also procedural. Advocacy is conducted according to rules of procedure that constitute a testing of substance.[15]

Thus, it appears that, far from endangering the essentials of the discipline, entering the marketplace has forcibly refocused the concerns of historians on the central questions which arise from studying the past and has given it new life in its ancient setting, the conflicting and fateful interests of the public world which drove Thucydides, Caesar, Gibbon, and a host of other men of affairs to write history. Although the issues surrounding the ethics of doing history are important, the arguments over the nature and meaning of the discipline itself are far more serious, especially in the sense that it is the public memory that makes social and personal life possible. In the next two chapters, we shall examine some of these arguments in two contexts: first, the fundamental changes which have occurred in the meaning of science and second, the way in which these changes must profoundly affect the discipline of history. On the basis of this discussion we propose a practicable model for the unification of public and academic history.

NOTES

1. Charles Phillips and Patricia Hogan, *The Wages of History* (Nashville, Tennessee: American Association for State and Local History, 1984), 25.
2. *Survey of the Historical Profession, Academia, 1981–82, Summary Report* (Washington: American Historical Association, 1984), 5.
3. *The Public Historian*, Vol. I, No. 1 (Fall, 1978), 52.
4. *Wages of History, 15–26.*
5. Lawrence B. DeGraff, Gregory Graves, G. Wesley Johnson and Robert W. Pomeroy III, compilers and eds., *Survey of the Historical Profession, Public Historians, 1980–81: Summary Report* (Washington: American Historical Association, 1981).
6. *Survey of the Historical Profession, Public History*, 16, 17. This report is 27 pages, with the first 20 pages devoted to numerical data and the last 6 pages providing samples of written responses.
7. Robert Kelley, "ANNOUNCEMENT, The Undergraduate Major in the HISTORY OF PUBLIC POLICY," September 1, 1983, unpublished.
8. *Educating Historians for Business* (Bloomington, Indiana: Organization of American Historians, 1983), 14.
9. New York University Department of History brochure describing its program.
10. Howard Green, "A Critique of the Professional Public History Movement," *Radical History Review*, 25 (1981), 169.
11. Richard E. Neustadt and Ernest R. May, *Thinking in Time: The Uses of History for Decision Makers* (New York: Free Press, 1986), 251.

12. Computed from the raw data of a survey of public history programs in the U.S. and Canada conducted by Barbara Howe in 1985.

13. Ronald C. Tobey, "The Public Historian as Advocate: Is Special Attention to Professional Ethics Necessary?," *The Public Historian*, Vol. VIII, No. 1 (Winter, 1986), 21–30.

14. H. L. A. Hart and A. M. Honoré, *Causation in the Law* (New York: Oxford University Press, 1959), 35–39, 147.

15. Tobey, *op. cit*, 25, 27.

Chapter 2

HISTORY AND SCIENCE: A DEBATE FROM THE PAST

There is a general crisis in the human sciences: they are all over-whelmed by the extent of the progress they have made. . . . All, some more consciously than others, are preoccupied with their position in relation to the monstrous body of research. . .[1]

Fernand Braudel

Since its appearance as an academic discipline, there have been recurrent questions about the purpose of history. Is history a science or an art? Does it have predictive value? Or is it a literary and humanistic excursion into distant times and esoteric places? What can it teach us about men, about life, about world order, about cosmic design? Are the accounts of the past dry records for their own sake, or can we learn something from their study? Does history repeat itself, and if so, in what patterns? Are men merely interested in providing for their own immortality by establishing the records of their own times, or can these records help us to improve our own societies? At root, these questions really ask about the value of communicating across the dimensions of time and cultures. What, for example, can we understand of the cave drawings of prehistoric men? How should we interpret the artifactual evidence of mummies, pyramids, and murals from ancient Egypt? How can we use or make sense of the epic poetry of Homer? Are these merely interesting evidences of bygone cultures, or do they speak to us in some meaningful way today?

While these examples may seem distant and irrelevant, they can be made less so by applying questions of the same form to more recent times and specific instances. What, for example, can we learn from studying the Renaissance? Do we do so merely to appreciate an earlier art form, or is there some application to the present? What also of the American past—the era of Reconstruction, the Great Depression, the Korean and Vietnam wars, the most recent stock market crash? When Robert McFarlane testified at the Iran-Contra hearings, he said in his opening statement: ". . . a solution to the fundamental problems . . . will require much more . . . reform of institutions and processes and, most important, . . . changes in the attitudes and behavior of the men and women who hold and exercise public power."[2] What can history teach us of these processes and how can it influence behavior and attitudes? If we understand the past better, can we use that knowledge? How can we use it?

Assuming for the moment that one might find some persuasive and incisive, if not uniform, answers to the question, "Why study history," there remains the related question of "how." For every answer to the first question—a question of purpose or end—there must be a means. What methods will enable the historian to transmit the necessary information about the past effectively? Obviously, such a question cannot be answered without first determining purpose. A methodology for history, therefore, is necessarily related to its purpose and value. In the course of this chapter, we intend to demonstrate that history has unexpected value, not only because memory is fundamental, but precisely because of the twin foundations of time and human experience upon which the discipline of history rests. We shall demonstrate that, contrary to common belief, these twin foundations, based upon assumptions of irreversible change and inescapable subjectivity, are completely consistent with twentieth-century findings in science and the philosophy of science and provide history with its depth and value as a discipline.

From the earliest recorded writings, men have made distinctions between that which has general and enduring value and application and that which provides singular, concrete knowledge. For Aristotle, poetry, like theoretical science, is " '. . . more philosophic and of graver import' than history" precisely because the former deals with the pervasive and the universal.[3] Historians from ancient times to the Renaissance struggled with this distinction, and attempted through their narratives and rhetoric to make history as "universal" as possible, designing lessons in morality, and distinguishing character types, generally oblivious to the temporal, cultural, and geophysical dimensions of their endeavor. History was perceived as a narrative art, whose purpose was to amuse and to teach and to reach toward general truths as exhibited in poetry and theoretical science.

Throughout the Middle Ages, Christian thinkers infused this universal vision of history with a theological design. The medieval ideal constituted a hierarchy of law governing creation, which linked eternal, revealed, natural, and human patterns. The all-powerful, infinite God of creation was the source of all meaning for man's otherwise confusing journey. The study of history could demonstrate God's purpose through human successes and failures as well as through natural catastrophes or periods of plenty. History was a means to better understand divine intent. Monastic chroniclers often devoted themselves to the collection of details, but these facts were always conceived of as part of a record to document God's purposes. In medieval times, the immense value and universal nature of history appeared obvious. History, like all other parts of life, was linked to the eternal and the metaphysical.

The first age of science, dominated by Copernican astronomy and Galilean physics, required historians to grapple seriously with the question of their purpose in at least two ways. First, if there were laws of nature, discoverable by human reason, were there also laws at work in human society? If so, could history help in the discovery of those laws? If not, could the study of history have any enduring value? Second, if these mathematically-definable laws of the physical universe actually explained natural events and could also predict them, what was the effect on the idea of divine causation? Were individuals no longer to be perceived as agents of God, controlled by Him for unknown divine purposes? Did they have free will? Were they able to shape events and have an impact upon the future? Could history be used to discover and explain such human action? This first scientific age forced historians to reevaluate fundamental issues of motivation, causation, and explanation.

With this reevaluation came a variety of responses. Some refused to give up the familiar and comforting theories of the past. An example is Bishop Bossuet of France, who long into the seventeenth century, continued to write that type of universal history which was designed to reveal God's hand through the success of divine absolute monarchy. More than a century before Bossuet, however, those like Machiavelli and Guicciardini used history to demonstrate "secondary" (or nondivine) causal patterns. Reflecting the all-consuming political unrest in Italy, they attempted to explain human political action and reaction. Machiavelli even tried to establish objective "rules" of political action which were totally divorced from moral considerations, and which could be demonstrated to be effective through the actions of a Cesare Borgia or a Francesco Sforza. Just as there were rules governing the natural universe, so too could there be rules governing man-made communities.[4]

One of the most thoughtful and provocative responses to the success of Renaissance physics came through the writings of Giambattista Vico. For him, history was fundamentally

different from natural science in its methods and proce-
dures. He perceived history as the record of men in civil
society and claimed its principles necessarily to be based on
" . . . the modifications of the human mind;" ". . . that which
can be known with certainty are particular events, laws, customs, and institutions."[5] Every people, every society, every
nation passes through stages of development; every culture
is therefore fluid. This *scienza* of History is ". . . a history of
human ideas, on which it seems the metaphysics of the human mind must proceed."[6] Rejecting René Descartes' claim
that an objective, uniform method of reason could be applied to establish certain knowledge of man's world, Vico
illustrated the cultural variety and temporal change in human society. History could help us to understand, but it
could not lead to universal truths, as in science. History must
remain an art based on the capacity to imaginatively recreate
the character of past ages; history was fundamentally different from the world of science.

Vico's insistence on the distinctive cultural variations in
customs, laws, and languages as well as on the constant flux
of time had little concrete impact on thought in his own
time. Most historians, throughout the mid-eighteenth century, perceived themselves as the philosophers and poets of
their day, revealing truths of universal value. By means of
history, they would provide men with knowledge of human
behavior and, therefore, knowledge of themselves: history
was a universal science of man's behavior and its consequences.[7] For most of these historians, there was no uncom-
fortable distinction between the world of science and the
historian's narrative art. Most thinkers could not or would
not grapple with the fundamental issues of time and change,
lest doing so undermined the importance of history.

Nevertheless, historians slowly came to recognize the importance of cultural variation and nonpolitical determinants

of human action. By the time of Voltaire, history became more than the deeds of its kings and generals as writers began to look at least superficially at social and economic issues and at broad cultural differences. As historians became more aware of these elements, they also became somewhat more focused, writing national histories rather than universal or general ones. In addition, they paid greater attention to historical sources and their verification, they adopted a secular approach, examining the "secondary" causes for human action, and they insisted on the "truth" of their findings, which, they claimed, distinguished them from their literary cohorts. In other words, they concluded that history was fundamentally different from poetry—and better—because it was based on verifiable, accurate sources. If history could not have universal truth, at least it could be based on identifiable "facts." To this degree, historians attempted to be scientific, which largely meant they tried to adopt an empirical approach. They founded the discipline of modern history, distinct from literature and poetry, yet still a narrative form. Its value was that it was an accurate portrayal, they claimed, of the people (or nation or culture) under study.[8]

The tremendous achievements of nineteenth century physics and biology led to a second age of science and to an all-pervasive "scientific ideal." Auguste Comte argued the possibility of a science of society through the creation of universal laws.[9] The new "truths" of science not only established universal laws which could be tested and replicated by detached human observers, but also took into account the process of evolution—of change. Darwin and his followers claimed universal laws of growth and development which could be scientifically demonstrated. This seemed to be a perfect model for historians. Applying the values of his age, Otto von Ranke believed that history was a tool for developing knowledge of an objective reality. In his very first book, *History of the Latin and Teutonic Nations*, published in 1824, he established the principle that historians should resist the temptation to express moral, political, or religious values, concentrating instead on presenting "what actually happened"—"wie es eigentlich gewesen."[10] The historian must be committed to accuracy and scrutiny of sources above all else. A school of German historians developed around von Ranke, which attempted to cut its ties with philosophy and literature, to adopt a critical method for the collection of facts, and to claim history as an academic discipline of verifiable objectivity.[11] The Rankean school entered the American universities in the 1870s through Johns Hopkins and Columbia, giving rise to the seminar, graduate education, and a steadily widening break between the public and the academy. History for the public remained a literary and narrative art in the hands of men of affairs like George Bancroft and Frances Parkman; history for the academy assumed a more "professional" audience which would be reached through scholarly and specialized journals or through university presses which would publish their ". . . detached, objective, more 'scientific' search for causes and relationships."[12] These professionals increasingly scorned the generalists within the field of history, as they used the specific facts of history to validate hypotheses from other disciplines and sought to demonstrate that history was one of those "value-free" or "value-neutral" disciplines which could claim to have scientific validity.[13]

Such conclusions were not reached without significant debate, a debate which was particularly sophisticated in the hands of philosophers. Over the past generation, most of the impetus for developing new methodologies has been derived from the need to cope with the epistemological bias of positivism, which assumes that the uncovering of objective regularities called natural laws will necessarily lead to simplicity and control. The works of Auguste Comte, appearing between the years 1830 and 1854, put forth the ideal that society could be explained and predicted by means of the application of the scientific method. His basic philosophic principle was that ". . . social phenomena are subject to natural laws, admitting of rational prevision," which establish both the conditions of order and progress in the universe. Instead of focusing on research into causes, which he concluded was both speculative and vain, he would seek to discover the natural laws which governed social and political organization, and would attempt to reduce them to the smallest possible number.[14] His interest was to establish a predictive model; his approach was based on Cartesian deductive principles. He was convinced that through his methodology, the "historical method" followed logically from the rules of positivist research, based on observation, experiment, and comparison. History was raised to new levels of precision. Comte's conviction was that

> . . . the new political philosophy restores to History all its scientific rights as a basis of wise social speculation. . . . In this case, so far from restricting the influence which human reason has ever attributed to history in political combinations, the new social philosophy increases it, radically and eminently. It asks from history something more than counsel and instruction to perfect conceptions which are derived from another source: it seeks its own general direction, through the whole system of historical conclusions.[15]

The basic issue was drawn: Could historians achieve the kind of results which scientists claimed for themselves? Could they, in fact, reduce social and political behavior to a set of laws, presumably mathematical in form?

As late nineteenth and twentieth century thinkers responded to the basic premises of positivism, some focused on the ways in which historians provide an explanation of events and some suggested patterns or models which should be used to explain adequately a historical event. While some of these thinkers were descriptive and some prescriptive, there was, nonetheless, general agreement that the concept of *explanation* in history was basic.[16] If historical explanation could be shown to be similar to or coincident with scientific explanation, then history could have predictive value and its importance in the modern world would be obvious.

Not all philosophers accepted the idea of a necessary relationship between objective laws and historical explanation. Some, like Croce and Collingwood admitted the irremediable methodological subjectivity of any study of human society. An early twentieth-century critic, Benedetto Croce, argued that the work of the historian was more closely related to that of artist than scientist. There was no such thing as a stark fact; rather, the documents of history must be interpreted and judged by the historian, who inevitably did so in conjunction with a present-minded interest. Max Weber despaired over the unbridgeable gap between scientific knowledge (the "Is") and ultimate moral norms (the "Ought").[17] R.G. Collingwood, whose now crucial *Idea of History* was published posthumously in 1946, distinguished between the "inside" and "outside" of an event, arguing that the events of history were fundamentally different from mere physical phenomena. He concluded:

> . . . the processes of nature are not historical processes and our knowledge of nature, though it may resemble history in certain superficial ways, e.g., by being chronological, is not historical knowledge.[18]

This statement by Collingwood is characteristic of the almost universal willingness by both scholars and the knowledgeable public to concede the claim by scientists that science, understood as the testing of hypotheses under controlled conditions for the purpose of uncovering physical laws and the prediction of events, is unique in the immense power of its ability to provide useful and exact knowledge of an objective physical world. Such an admission had the effect of dividing knowledge into two kinds: scientific and humane. Only the first was rigorously demonstrable, while the second, though useful, was weak and unreliable. This division into two different kinds of inquiry with completely different methodologies necessarily producing completely different and conflicting forms of knowledge, made it appear that the search for knowledge itself was not and could never become a unified enterprise. By 1958, Peter Winch, in *The Idea of a Social Science and Its Relation to Philosophy*, proclaimed the fundamental conceptual disparity between social and natural disciplines and attacked the assumed conflict between philosophy and studies of society.[19] Others, like Karl Popper categorically rejected the hypothesis of absolute knowledge in any discipline. For him, not even scientific knowledge could conform to the rigors of logical positivism. Nonetheless, according to Popper, scientific knowledge is progressive, while the most we can expect from the theoretical social sciences, is "... to explain how the unintended consequences of our intentions and actions arise, and what kind of consequences arise if people do this that or the other in a certain social situation," thereby raising our consciousness about future choices.[20] Throughout the twentieth century then, a consistent strain of thought has differentiated the discipline of history from that of science. In so doing, philosophers and historians were constantly forced to *justify* history as a discipline able to produce knowledge, as distinct from mere opinion.

Some, however, continued to pursue the line of reasoning begun by Comte to include history in the domain of the sciences. In the process, many of them modified the program by which they tied predictive laws to history. Carl Hempel argued that general laws of explanation and prediction had analogous functions in history and the natural sciences. Examining the "logic of discovery," he argued that the underlying *process* is identical. It is, he acknowledged, more difficult to develop unambiguously the initial conditions and hypotheses necessary to establish a general law in history; therefore, we can expect "explanation *sketches*" as analyses of historical events.[21] In basic agreement was Ernest Nagel, who rejected the notion that, on the one hand, the theoretical sciences were attempting "to establish abstract general laws for indefinitely repeatable processes" (a nomothetic science) while on the other history attempted ". . . to understand the unique and nonrecurrent" (an ideographic science). His conclusion was that

> The explanatory premises in history, as in the natural sciences, include a number of implicitly assumed laws, as well as many explicitly (though usually incompletely) formulated singular statements of initial conditions.[22]

Years later, he continued to assert that scientists, like humanists, are members of social institutions and intellectual communities, and are thereby capable of tacitly subscribing to current false assumptions. Scientists and humanists share a "common temper of mind."[23] While philosophers like William Dray, Charles Frankel, and Alan Donagan questioned the validity of Hempel's "covering laws," the debate between Collingwood and Hempel remained basic.

Fundamental to this philosophic debate was the issue of objectivity. The social and natural sciences were distinguished from each other on the basis of behavior governed respectively by the prescriptive rules of society or by the descriptive laws of nature. Subversive and unpredictable, "human nature" was contrasted with the docility and pre-

dictability of "nature." Man and nature, observer and observed, subjective and objective, unscientific and scientific
were increasingly distinguished categorically. Positivists used
their canons of objectivity to separate completely the ob-
server/subject from the observed/object. The scientist was
described as value-neutral or even value-free.

Unfortunately for the positivists' visionary universe, Darwin and successors in biology, anthropology, psychology,
and linguistics raised problems which cannot be so easily put
aside. There are also nagging doubts that the scientist can
actually operate in a thoroughly objective or even disinterested manner. In 1953, Richard Rudner published a paper
entitled "The Scientist *qua* Scientist Makes Value Judgments."[24] In the laboratory, every scientist, whether physicist
or psychologist, must make value judgments in accepting and
rejecting any hypothesis. The crucial point is that the weight
of evidence which leads one scientist to accept a given hypothesis is insufficient for another. The difference between
the two is a judgment of value. Consequently, scientists constantly make value judgments, forcing the conclusion that
scientists and science are not value-neutral, and therefore
cannot be objective. This evident conclusion flies in the face
of generally accepted ideas about the nature of science.

Hempel raised yet another problem involving the objectivity of science: the fact that the form of scientific validation
contains an inescapable and devastating error in logic called
the fallacy of affirming the consequent. Here what may be
called the faith of scientific empiricism becomes apparent.
Any given hypothesis logically implies specific test results,
but the results do not and cannot logically validate the truth
of the hypothesis in question.

Suppose the hypothesis is put forward that all dogs are
mortal (p implies q). As long as no immortal dogs are discovered, we can accept the hypothesis, at least provisionally,

because the test results have followed the requirement that for every p there must follow a q. Of course, if we knew of one existent immortal dog, like Cerberus, the hypothesis would fail. The problem arises if we try to affirm the consequent, that q implies p—that only the dogs die. Dead men, lilies, mackerel and beetles confirm what the rule of deduction has already forbidden: the particular conclusion cannot evidence the universal premise. Therefore, the fact that tests of hypotheses come out as expected does not logically validate the hypotheses themselves.

All that remains to support any hypothesis is the faith that because the test results continue to happen as expected (dogs keep on dying), we have *some* basis in believing the validity of the hypothesis. We have learned to believe, with the scientists, that repetition is an indication of the presence of regularity in a lawful universe. However, we have found no way to determine at what point in a sequence of repetitions regularity replaces coincidence. This inability to give meaning to regularity makes certain that a subjective judgment of sufficient evidence determines the acceptance or rejection of hypotheses. While historical generalization is not the same idea as regularity, it serves an identical purpose for historians by giving regularity to events on the basis of an equally subjective judgment about the sufficiency of evidence for it.

Finally, the debate between those who perceive history as science and those who perceive it as art—a debate which hinges, as we have shown, on the central issue of objectivity—fails to consider the curious status of mathematics and of logic, generally. On the one hand, mathematics make science possible. On the other, it is nonempirical, untestable, a consequence of introspection, rule-governed, judged aesthetically, metaphorical and symbolic. All these characteristics the positivist—and most scientists—would avoid as unscientific and value-charged. Since scientists and philosophers of science usually insist that meaning is an objective category and refuse to consider the more likely position that meaning constitutes a relationship between the observer and the observed, they are unable to provide a model of complexity adequate to the needs of an inquiry in which objectivity is but one controversial methodological issue.

In short, the movement of ideas which began with the apparently simple and unobjectionable assertion in the nineteenth century that science is by nature objective and which created such pairs of opposites as art/science, subject/object, value-charged/value-free and the like has become steadily more complicated and has focused more and more on the nature of science itself in such a way that objectivity itself has come to seem less and less defensible. For some scientists, it has even become undesirable as a goal of inquiry precisely because it proposes to divorce human experience from explanations about the universe and seems to deny that science is only one of a number of significant human activities.

For their part, historians, motivated by the need to justify and legitimate their discipline in the face of scientific disparagement, have themselves written extensively on the nature of history. This need arose not only from the challenge of the developing social sciences, which seemed more able to adopt a convincingly objective tone than historians, but also from the dislocation and barbarism of two world wars which led them to ask difficult questions about the assumptions of their discipline. If the presumably civilized West had behaved so badly, what did its history now mean? Had there in fact been real human progress? Was historical knowledge applicable to events at all if two such gross events had not been easily and generally forecast by professional historians? Generally, what were the values essential for the study of history?

In France, England, and the United States, an extensive literature developed to examine the purpose and methodology of history. While very different in their particulars, they shared a common view that the historian could and must utilize the social sciences, and would necessarily write for other professionals. While a few unique individuals could move back and forth between the world of general popular history and the demanding needs of professional scholarship,[26] most accepted the need to narrow their focus in order to test a hypothesis through an "objective" methodology. The broader public was lost, as was the notion of history as a literary art. For the professional historian, it seemed more important to justify the discipline within the twentieth-century world of natural and social scientific theory.

Nevertheless, the ancient concern with time and change continued to produce alternatives to the narrowed scientific focus. One enormously influential model for doing so developed in France during the 1920s. The Annales school, created by Marc Bloch and Lucien Febvre, was founded on a perspective which viewed history as an integrative discipline of great depth and enormous breadth. Strongly critical of the notion that positivist science could enrich history, and contemptuous of those who would revere the "fact" or "event" for its own sake, those of the Annales school advocated problem-oriented history. But the problems which should interest historians had to be formulated with creative insight and with sensitivity to cultural and temporal diversities. There could be no determinism in history; indeed, there could not even be any meaningful definition of history, because as Lucien Febvre and Marc Bloch agreed, ". . . any definition is a prison."[27] Specialization in history had led to the creation of rigid categories, to an idolization of facts through the German seminar method, and to world views which were unbending and unyielding. No doubt inspired by the turmoil of their ". . . age of upheavals, uncertainty and demolition,"[28] these founders of a new school of history insisted that history could be more meaningfully conceptualized. For them, the narrative of events was the last stage in a process, which began first with an understanding of the geophysical environment, and proceeded to an appreciation of the economic and social environment, in an effort to establish an appropriate setting for the facts. The historian must be a creative investigator, alive to the spirit of the times and culture under investigation, and open to the notion that " 'There are no necessities, but everywhere possibilities' in the relation between man and his environment."[29]

For the Annalistes, history was fundamentally different from the social sciences, because of its concern with time and its unique view of structure. In a tribute to Marc Bloch, who was mercilessly killed by the Nazis in 1944, Lucien Febvre notes Bloch's view of historical time:

> History does not think merely in 'human' terms. Its natural setting is that of duration. It is indeed the science of men, but of men placed in time. Time, continuous but also standing for perpetual change. 'The great problems of historical research arise out of the antitheses between these two attributes.'[30]

That fundamental concern with time led Fernand Braudel, a leading historian and thinker in our own times, to formulate the specific differences between historians and other social scientists on the notion of time and structure. The historian, he writes, must be constantly aware of ". . . the plurality of social time."[31] There are at least three different notions of historical time: the short term (with its emphasis on the individual and the event), the cyclical (encompassing anything from a decade to a half-century), and the long term (which incorporates centuries). For Braudel, the historian's traditional focus on the short term distorts reality. Sharing Febvre's view that the historian must rise above the event, he argued that the long-term lens was most revealing for historical analysis. This would lead to a concept of time that is both "mathematical and creative."[32]

By its very nature, time could not be static. The historian had to realize that time, itself, was constantly moving on. Therefore, the historian's concept of structure was likewise fundamentally different from that of the social scientist. Braudel writes:

> To students of society, structure means organization, coherence, a set of fairly stable relationships between social reality and the body of society. To historians like ourselves, while structure does, of course, mean an assembly of parts, a framework, it signifies more particularly a reality which survives through long periods of time and is only slowly eroded. Some particularly long-lived structures become the stable elements of generation after generation: they resist the course of history and therefore determine its flow. Other structures disintegrate more quickly. But all structures act both as foundations and obstacles.[33]

In other words, structure and time interact in unique ways, and it is the task of the historian to understand and explain that interaction. Only with the long-term view of time can one get at the most important issues of cultural change; only through the *longue dureé* can one understand fundamental structural changes which explain the evolution of man *in* society. Thus, the Annalistes would have us consider such frameworks (or structures) as the geographical, the psychological/emotional, and the cultural and their impact on individual and social consciousness. For example, as early as 1941, Lucien Febvre wrote that one needed to understand the *sensibilités* of human beings in social systems: how emotions affected a climate of opinion, perhaps even becoming institutions of a sort themselves. Consider, he suggests, the emotional impact of night/day, dark/light, winter/summer, food/scarcity on the psychology of medieval man. Did such conditions not create a fundamentally distinct *mentalité* and *sensibilité* from later historical periods?[34] Must we not study medieval history with those perceptions in view? Braudel, writing in 1958, understood that scientific notions of the universe had themselves undergone change, affecting the *mentalités* of civilized man, as the Aristotelian system gave way to the Newtonian, and much later, to the Einsteinian.[35] Thus, the historian limits his contribution if he tries to adopt the approach of the social sciences, which study a single structure or have an absolute notion of time.

While the historian is not another social scientist, he can of course, benefit from the techniques and tools of various kinds of specialists. In particular, the interpretive tools of linguistics (the understanding of words in relation to one another), iconography (the study of images in the visual arts), and literature (the study of forms of writing), as well as the insights of geographers, sociologists, and psychologists help to inform the historian in his monumental task.[36]

Obviously, the historian cannot become informed in all these technical areas. (Indeed, the thought is all the more overwhelming when one considers the growing technical sophistication of the social science disciplines). The Annalistes, therefore, urged the teamwork approach, envisioning the creation of "history laboratories," "well-coordinated investigations," and "flexible research directors."[37] Such research teams would be able to pool their diverse skills, develop the significant questions, identify the available kinds of data, estimate expenditures, establish staff, process the findings, and present them to the public.[38] Their sources would not only be the traditional documents of moral conduct (available in archival collections), but would extend to artistic materials from the plastic and musical arts, literary documents, and "Words, signs, landscapes, titles, the layout of fields, weeds, eclipses of the moon, bridles, analysis of stones by geologists and of metal swords by chemists, in a word, anything which, belonging to man, depends on man, serves him, expresses him and signifies his presence, activity, tastes and forms of existence."[39] Such a vision would, indeed, save the historian from scurrying after the individual fact, and would elevate the historian to the revered position of the deepest student of man in society. As we shall see, such a vision of history also formulates a practical integrative model—one which should be able to bridge the present gap between the academy and the public, and one which should provide guidance for reintegrating the discipline of history.

In the postwar era, as scientific technology seemed to provide predictable comforts and outcomes for the future, historians as well as social scientists sought to demonstrate their value along the continuum of determinism. Clearly, historians could not compete. In the United States, especially, the scientific ideal of predictability became paramount, and the behavioral sciences of psychology, sociology, and anthropology seemed to displace history in their ability to formulate useful concepts to explain man and his society.[40] The conceptual synthesis of the Annales school, which developed between the 1920s and 1940s, was accepted by American historians in the 1940s and early 1950s, but was increasingly replaced by a social-scientific ideal in the 1950s and 1960s.

Immediately after World War II, the Committee on Historiography of the Social Science Research Council (including such leading historians as Charles Beard, Shepard B. Clough, Thomas Cochran, Louis Gottschalk and Merle Curti), published a study entitled *Theory and Practice in Historical Study: A Report of the Committee on Historiography*. An outgrowth of a 1952 conference, this publication summarized several years of discussion on the nature of historical thought and writing. In his introductory essay, Charles Beard gave expression to the fundamental dilemma which is still with us—one which is at the heart of the success of the Public History movement:

> History is treated as having little or no relation to the conduct of practical affairs and yet is constantly employed in efforts to validate the gravest policies, proposals, contentions, and dogmas advanced for adoption in respect of domestic and foreign affairs. . . . History can scarcely be at the same time a useless old almanac and the ultimate source of knowledge and 'laws' for demonstrating the invincible validity of policies proposed or already in practice.[41]

Recognizing that social scientists were succeeding in applying their skills outside the academy, Beard called for a "reconsideration" of the place and meaning of history. Like those of the Annales school, Beard viewed history as fundamental and called ancillary to it such disciplines as economics, politics, sociology, anthropology, psychology, ethics, and esthetics because all such ways of knowing are aspects of what he calls "history-as-actuality."[42] Without the reality of history, concepts employed by those in the social sciences become mere abstractions, devoid of content. Terms like democracy, political man, rational man, or capitalism, have no meaning apart from history, and likewise, cannot be seen as elements in independent or free-moving disciplines. Thus, history remains the great synthesizer of human knowledge, incorporating the other social sciences and allowing them to check their abstractions against the knowledge of history. Indeed, there is even an empirical relationship between the disciplines. History, in effect, becomes the data against which the hypotheses of the social sciences can be verified. According to Beard, ". . . history, itself, as actuality, passes judgment on the validity of propositions in the humanistic sciences."[43] Thus, history is not akin to science, but in its application it becomes a fundamental part of the empirical method of scientists in their search for verifiable proof of their findings.

A second report of the Committee on Historiography was published in 1954. Entitled *The Social Sciences in Historical Study*, this report noted the shift of the "climate of opinion" with the efforts of historians to form amalgamations with other disciplines.[44] Indeed, in the minds of those on the Social Science Research Council, history was now regarded as one of the social sciences. This later report focuses on the concepts which can best be employed from the social sciences, the problems of historical analysis, and the unique ways in which the historian, as social scientist, deals with change.

The authors call for a greater use of theory as a means to suggest problems, establish organizational categories, and supply hypotheses. They are not interested in the "non-operational" theories of those like Spengler and Toynbee, but in "operational" theories which can be proved either false or correct through empirical evidence.[45] History, it is argued, is no less capable of proceeding as a social science than any other discipline. In a critical chapter on "History among the Social Sciences," the *PROCESS* of research is shown to be universal for both the social and natural sciences:

> In historical research the process of inquiry ordinarily begins, not with testing of hypotheses deduced from a general theory, but with a problem of interpretation presented by a certain body of empirical material. Whether in the natural or the social sciences, the procedure is the same. Confronted with such a problem, the investigator draws up a series of tentative working hypotheses, derived from his general knowledge of phenomena of this type and his familiarity with relevant theoretical developments, and then proceeds to test these hypotheses against his observations.[46]

History is in this view scientific both in its descriptive function (because it establishes credible evidence—the facts) and in its explanatory function (because it analyzes how and why events occurred). It is a mistaken notion of science to consider evidence as permanently transfixed in time. Even scientifically derived data is part of a process, ". . . the precipitates of the interplay of dynamic factors operating through preceding events and probably continuing to operate through succeeding events."[47] In the final chapter on "Problems of Historical Analysis," Samuel H. Brockunier and Bert Lowenberg summarize the similarities between the social and physical sciences, insisting on the impossibility of achieving total knowledge and complete predictability:

> In all science, social as well as physical, much useful theory and many fascinating explorations do not yield complete knowledge. In the analysis of causation the true scientific spirit involves the determination of the more or less, the prediction of probabilities rather than certainties, the conscientious search for techniques to overcome the limitations of the evidence, and a willingness to admit that sometimes we do not have the answers.[48]

Despite this synthetic framework, this analysis of the relation of history to the social sciences focuses in its detail on specific concepts and hypotheses taken from the social sciences which can be useful to the historian. From anthropology come the concepts of culture and personality structure; from sociology—values, group analyses, social norms, roles and functions, ideologies; from the field of demography, the historian can learn population analysis through studies of family and household, urban and rural communities, immigrant and native groups; psychology provides explanations of national, individual and group behaviors; political science offers theories of power and policy making; economics is rich with analyses of natural resources, agricultural production, aggregates, and the nature of exchange. These concepts, terms, or hypotheses from other social sciences would enable historians to apply their skills in the world at large. The assumption was that history ". . . is not exclusively chaos or chance: a degree of observable order and pattern, or partially predictable regularity, exists in human behavior."[49] The historical method, then, is proposed as follows:

> . . . the historian is concerned with finding a valid explanation of particular sequences of events; he develops this explanation by relating the concrete sequence to underlying tendencies and processes of change in the structure of the society and culture. He starts with the unique historical situation and, while setting his stage, states his problem. He then analyzes the structure of the situation at several different but related levels—the immediate context, the groups involved, the structure of the society, and the cultural tradition—with particular emphasis on the processes and potentialities of change at each of these levels and how they influenced individual behavior. His conclusion, if his analysis is successful, is a generalized statement of the nature and meaning of the sequence of events in this particular culture, and an *explanation* of the sequence in terms of the causal influences affecting it.[50]

In short, by the 1950s, the leading historians in America had conceptualized a role for history as the queen of the social sciences, but, at the same time, had forced it into a rigid mold. While not rejecting the approach of those in the Annales school, they had limited the potential for historical imagination by proposing too close an alliance with the restrictive methodologies of social science. In the graduate schools, this approach would lead to narrower and narrower analysis of issues in the effort to "prove" a valid thesis. In the process, the public would become less and less interested.

What occurred was that historians and other social scientists adopted a fundamental misconception about science: the positivist view that science, through the application of appropriate conditions and laws, could provide answers to questions about the future. Because it was clear that social scientists, more than historians, had the "models" which corresponded to the "laws" of science, they also claimed that they had something useful to market. Historians could choose either to adopt these models or to admit that they did not have anything so marketable. Richard Hofstadter, a champion of the view that social scientific methodology could enrich history, admitted in 1956 that historians could not adapt themselves easily to the scientific ideal, since they could not ". . . conduct experiments, or, strictly speaking, make predictions. . . . "[51] Nonetheless, those like Richard Hofstadter, David Potter, John Higham, C. Vann Woodward, and Lee Benson made their reputation by applying social scientific models of political culture, economic abundance, human psychology and party analysis to the experience of history. In the process, they isolated a significant strain of the American historical experience, and demonstrated clearly the impact of social scientific categorization on the insight of the historian. What was often lost in this orientation was the diversity of the historical experience. In the interests of isolating a significant strain, and demonstrating their union with social scientists, historians often gave up their distinguishing characteristic as synthesizers of disparate strains of activity and thought within the dimension of time. As good social scientists, it was necessary to isolate a subsystem with a fair degree of accuracy.[52]

At the same time, despite these tendencies toward quantification and objectification, the old, comforting image of history as a Greek Muse—of history as a literary art of immense value—refused to die. This is the history which continues to absorb the broader public, both within and outside the setting of the university. Thinking of history as a story to be told and understood, many university professors, who would never adopt this approach in their own research endeavors, teach students this "story" of the past. Their orientation is to events; their periodization relies on the established divisions of Ancient, Medieval, and Modern—along with the subdivisions of Renaissance, Reformation, Early Modern (in the European dimension) and Colonial, Early National, and Reconstruction periods (in the American dimension.) Novelty lies less in the classification of events and more in its ability to humanize men to moral and cultural issues. The textbook model continues to be an attempt to synthesize history. To the extent that the public outside the university is attracted (and there is evidence that it is), it is to this variant of history. To the extent that this type of history continues to have its advocates, from both a professional but skeptical cadre of historians as well as a broad-based public, the nagging question of the nature of history— whether an art or a science—remains.

Yet the question and the distinction it embodies are themselves beginning to lose force. If objectivity, the presumed hallmark of science, is impossible in particle physics, which describes matter in its finest grain, because Heisenberg's Uncertainty Principle forbids any act of measurement which does not disturb the universe, then the inability of historians to achieve objectivity is, at worst, no more damaging to them than it is to physicists. At the least, we may expect that recent changes in the way science is perceived will offer historians an unexpected validity for their discipline.

NOTES

1. Fernand Braudel, "Time, History, and the Social Sciences," in Fritz Stern, ed., *The Varieties of History* (N.Y.: Random House, 1972), 404.
2. *The Washington Post*, May 12, 1987, A14.
3. Baldwin, Charles S. ed. *Aristotle's Poetics*, trans. Ingram Bywater (New York: Macmillan Company, 1930), 18.
4. Niccolo Machiavelli, *The Prince and The Discourses*, trans. Luigi Ricci (N.Y.: Random House, 1950), 8, 18, 22, 24, 30, 318, passim.
5. Giambattista Vico, *The New Science*, trans. J. Bergin and M. Fisch (N.Y.: Doubleday, 1961), 53.

6. *Ibid.*, 62.

7. See, for example, John Bennett Black, *The Art of History: A Study of Four Great Historians of the Eighteenth Century* (N.Y.: Russel and Russel, Inc., 1965), 7, 15ff. For analyses of sixteenth and early seventeenth century assumptions about history, see George Huppert, *The Idea of Perfect History* (Chicago: University of Illinois Press, 1970); Donald R. Kelley, *Foundations of Modern Historical Scholarship* (N.Y.: Columbia University Press, 1970).

8. Phyllis K. Leffler, "The 'Histoire Raisonnée,' 1660–1720: A Pre-Enlightenment Genre," *Journal of the History of Ideas*, Vol. XXXVII, No. 2 (April-June, 1976), 219–240.

9. Harriet Martineau, ed., *The Positive Philosophy of Auguste Comte* (3 vols; London: George Bell and Sons, 1896); for a more concise statement of Comte's principles, see Auguste Comte, *Introduction to Positive Philosophy*, ed., & tr. Frederick Ferré (N.Y.: Bobbs-Merrill Co., 1970).

10. Leopold von Ranke, *The Secret of World History: Selected Writings on the Art and Science of History*, ed. & introduction by Roger Wines (N.Y.: Fordham University Press, 1981), 7. For his most famous statement about the role of the historian, see *Ibid.*, 56–59.

11. Stern, *Varieties of History*, 16.

12. Richard Hofstadter, "History and Sociology in the United States," in Seymour Lipset and Richard Hofstadter, ed., *Sociology and History: Methods* (N.Y.: Basic Books, 1968), 5.

13. *Theory and Practice in Historical Study: A Report of the Committee on Historiography* [Bulletin 54] (New York: Social Science Research Council, 1946), 23–25, 31.

14. Martineau, *The Positive Philosophy of Auguste Comte*, II, 218.

15. *Ibid.*, 256–257.

16. Patrick Gardiner, *Theories of History* (Illinois: The Free Press, 1959), 269.

17. Richard J. Bernstein, *Beyond Objectivism and Relativism: Science, Hermeneutics, and Praxis* (Philadelphia: University of Pennsylvania Press, 1985), 14; Max Weber, " 'Objectivity' in Social Science and Social Policy," in *On the Methodology of the Social Sciences*, ed. and trans. by E.A. Shils and H.A. Finch (Free Press, 1949).

18. Collingwood, R.G., *The Idea of History* (New York: Oxford University Press, 1956), 302.

19. Peter Winch, *The Idea of Social Science and its Relation to Philosophy* (New York: Humanities Press, 1958), 1–2.

20. Karl R. Popper, *Conjectures and Refutations: The Growth of Scientific Knowledge* (N.Y.: Basic Books, 1962), 125. For a further discussion of Popper, see below, pp. 71–72.
21. Carl G. Hempel, "The Function of General Laws in History," in *The Journal of Philosophy*, Vol. XXXIX, No. 2 (January 15, 1942), 35, 42.
22. Ernest Nagel, "Some Issues in the Logic of Historical Analysis," *Scientific Monthly*, Vol. LXXIV, No. 3 (March 1952), 162–169.
23. Ernest Nagel, *Teleology Revisited and Other Essays in the Philosophy and History of Science* (N.Y.: Columbia University Press, 1979), 13, 27.
24. Richard Rudner, "The Scientist *Qua* Scientist Makes Value Judgments," *Philosophy of Science*, Vol. 20, No. 1 (January, 1953), 1–6.
25. Carl G. Hempel, *Philosophy of Natural Science* (N.Y.: Prentice-Hall, 1966), 6–9.
26. Hofstadter, *Sociology and History*, 7.
27. Peter Burke, ed., *A New Kind of History: From the Writings of Febvre* (New York: Harper and Row, 1973), 31.
28. *Ibid.*
29. *Ibid.*, x, xi.
30. *Ibid.*, 32.
31. Braudel, "Time, History, and the Social Sciences," in *Varieties of History*, 406.
32. *Ibid.*, 408, 425.
33. *Ibid.*, 411.
34. Burke, ed., *A New Kind of History*, xv, 13–15.
35. Braudel, "Time, History, and the Social Sciences," in *Varieties of History*, 412.
36. Burke, ed., *A New Kind of History*, xii, 1–11, 20–23; Braudel, *Ibid.*, 411.
37. *A New Kind of History*, 32–33.
38. *Ibid.*
39. *Ibid.*, 24, 34.
40. David M. Potter, *People of Plenty: Economic Abundance and the American Character* (Chicago: U. of Chicago Press, 1954), xv.
41. *Theory and Practice in Historical Study*, 5.
42. *Ibid.*, 7.
43. *Ibid.*, 7–10, Quoted material, p. 10.
44. *The Social Sciences in Historical Study* [Bulletin 64] (N.Y.: Social Science Research Council, 1954), 13.
45. *Ibid.*, 28.
46. *Ibid.*, 29.

47. *Ibid.*, 88.
48. *Ibid.*, 89.
49. *Ibid.*, 95.
50. *Ibid.*, 104–105.
51. Richard Hofstadter, "History and the Social Sciences," in *Varieties of History*, 367.
52. It is interesting that David Potter, by the early 1970s, was pleading the case that history cannot be scientific, and should not attempt to be, because of the critical value of human judgment which the historian must apply. See Don E. Fehrenbacher, ed., *History and American Society: Essays of David M. Potter* (N.Y.: Oxford University Press, 1973), 28–47.

Chapter 3

THE METHODOLOGICAL VALUE OF HISTORY

For centuries the debate over the value of history has been cast in terms of its objectivity. That which is objective is that which is governed by laws, predictable, universally valid, and independent of time. The model for this standard of objectivity was drawn from the dualism of Descartes and became scientific doctrine in the nineteenth century. Try as they might, philosophers and historians had grave difficulty justifying the seriousness of the discipline of history when it so obviously dealt with the subjective and temporal. The standards for "scientific" truth appeared to be of a higher sort than those for "artistic" or "moral" or "historical" truths.

Such a conception of scientific order has had a profound impact on both the formulation of history as a discipline and for its acceptance as a study with value in the modern world. Scientific techniques appear to provide answers, to unlock doors to the future of critical issues in such areas as energy, medicine, and military predominance. We continue to believe that this world of science is really objective, orderly, rational, and infinitely repeatable. Accepting this simplistic view of scientific predictability, social scientists have argued that their own disciplines provide predictive models for understanding individual and group behaviors. Time and again, historians have been frustrated by their inability to make such claims for their discipline.

Within the past twenty or twenty-five years, scientists themselves have begun to question the grandiose claims

made for the precision and predictive ability of science. In
addition, inquiry has sought to move beyond the humanist-
positivist debate, and to frame issues in new ways that will
not simply recast the issues in terms of "objectivism" and
"relativism."[1]

As scientists and philosophers participate in this ongoing
argument, the role of history takes on new relevance. In
what follows, we will attempt to explain this changing conceptualization of science and its significance for the discipline of history. In order to demonstrate why the work of
the historian was devalued in the past and why it should
once again become a methodological model for explaining
human conduct, we shall review the position held by science
from the time of the first scientific revolution to the present
day. This analysis will illustrate the development over time
of similar epistemological premises held by both scientists
and historians. It is this shared epistemology which brings
the discipline of history back to center stage and demonstrates its utility in the world of affairs. It is this surprising
and unexpected agreement about the *basis* and the *process*
for achieving knowledge that justifies history as a discipline.
As we shall explain, the study of history is not merely an
elite training ground for classically educated people; it is a
discipline utilizing a process of inquiry which demonstrates
change over time, and which forces examination of complexity rather than simplicity, of frequent disorder as well
as order. It is the understanding and skills learned through
the study of history which are most indispensable for dealing
with the modern world.

SCIENTIFIC CONCEPTIONS OF WORLD ORDER
AND HISTORY

In the sixteenth and seventeenth centuries, "modern" science proposed to provide a picture of nature that was exact,

correct, and complete. This goal was to be achieved by observing nature objectively. For Galileo and those who succeeded him, objectivity meant making distinctions between the independent reality of primary qualities—matter, motion, and position—and the incorrigible subjectivity of secondary qualities—sense perception, feeling and, above all, value. Objectivity was to be reached by the simple act of wrenching human personality out of nature. This proposal necessarily meant that an objective picture of nature removed from it the persons who made it, a contradiction of perverse implications, among them the implausible conclusion made by the celebrated molecular biologist and Nobel Prize winner, Jacques Monod, that nature is alien to life, especially to human life:

> Man must at last finally awaken from his millenary dream; and in doing so, awake to his total solitude, his fundamental isolation. Now does he realize at last that, as a gypsy, he lives on the boundary of an alien world. A world deaf to his music, just as indifferent to his hopes as it is to his sufferings and his crimes.[2]

As Monod makes clear, objectivity as a necessary condition of scientific knowledge makes historical knowledge both impossible and irrelevant for two reasons: its subject matter, human life, has no reality and its methodology is incorrigibly subjective. Human experience, the essential foundation upon which the discipline of history rests, has no meaning in an "objective" universe.

The second foundation for history, as Braudel well understands, is the dimension of time. We must therefore consider how the classical scientist deals with issues of time and change. For the traditional physicist, the universe is understood as a dynamic system whose only variables are coordinates and momenta. It is the science of trajectories in which particles move through space and collide in accordance with physical laws. Positions change, but substances do not and matter remains unchanging throughout the whole of space and time. As these unchanging particles move, their relationships are described by the science of dynamics first formalized by Newton and later put in its most elegant form as a simple mathematical function called the Hamiltonian, in which the whole of the physical universe is interpreted by equations derived from it. The Hamiltonian, named after the distinguished nineteenth century mathematician William Rowland Hamilton, is expressed as $H(p[momentum], q[coordinates])$, and describes the dynamics of any physical system completely. All our knowledge of the physical universe can be put in the form of H. The Hamiltonian represents the triumph of the mathematization of nature and it stands as one of the most powerful achievements in science. It also results in the expulsion of human concerns from nature.

In this theoretically completely describable universe, time does not exist in the sense we experience it. This is so because the equations derived from the Hamiltonian are reversible in such a way that time inversion is mathematically the equivalent of velocity inversion. Nature is able, therefore, to run either forward or backward in time. For the physicist, for example, it is possible to run "Gone with the Wind" both forward and backward and have it make perfect scientific sense, in either direction, but at a loss, of course, of plot, characterization, emotion, society, history, and the meaning of science itself. Even Einstein, shortly before his death and half a century after the discovery of the relativity which undermined this Newtonian conception of time, could say with complete conviction:

> For us convinced physicists the distinction between past, present and future is an illusion, although a persistent one.[3]

Time, then, in the one-directional sense experienced by man, is absolutely denied by the assumptions of classical dynamics in science.

The importance of the above analysis lies not only in the fact that scientists generally, not just physicists, assume the necessity of objectivity and the mechanical forms of classical dynamics, but that the educated world generally does so as well. In particular, the consumers in the market for academically-based knowledge continue to accept this view of world order. They believe, in other words, in the Newtonian formulation that if the initial states of any system are known, the application of mathematical laws will produce either explanation of past events or predictions of future ones, and that the procedure to produce either is identical. Moreover, there is an assumption that "nature" around us is orderly and rational. Our everyday activities imply a perfect confidence in the universality of the laws of nature. Even if we observe some event which seems to us utterly mysterious, we remain persuaded that our experts' ignorance is only provisional—that the event only appears unlawful, and that its regularity will be discovered sooner or later.

It is upon such assumptions that social scientists base their claims of validity and significance. The social sciences seek predictability, in the guise of laws of human behavior; they claim a certain timelessness in the application of those laws; they argue for the essential objectivity of their pursuit. Confronted with such a world view, the historian is put at a great disadvantage. His emphasis on interpretation, human experience, the importance of time (and death), the ambiguity, multiplicity and unpredictability of complex events, and even the action of chance at the most critical moments, seems to leave him with no distinctive claim to useful knowledge. Even with the addition of cliometrics, sociology, psychohistory, anthropology, and political science, historians remain at a fundamental disadvantage. The classical view of world order, with its denial of both time and complexity, leaves historians with the dilemma of either becoming "relevant" by borrowing expediently from the social sciences, or upholding the integrity of history and accepting the fate of humanist irrelevance.

In the early nineteenth century, however, just as the Newtonian system seemed triumphant, Baron Jean Joseph Fourier formulated a law governing the propagation of heat, which became a significant threat to Newton's law of gravity.[4] The threat was contained in the idea that an irreversible process existed in nature, which if accepted meant that future scientists would need to calculate the erosions of time as well as physical dynamics. Building upon the work of Fourier, the later nineteenth century saw the creation of a science of thermodynamics, with its two elements of heat and energy. The work of Sadi Carnot, James Prescott Joule, Julius Robert von Mayer, and Hermann Ludwig Ferdinand von Helmholtz led to the formulation both of the second law of thermodynamics and the principle of conservation of energy. Their basic problems centered around loss of energy, conversion of potential energy into kinetic energy, and on the concept of entropy. This concept was introduced in 1865 by Rudolf Julius Emanuel Clausius. He was attempting to discover how energy can be conserved in physiochemical transformations, even though they cannot be reversed. The measure of the amount of energy that escapes from a system during a natural process he termed entropy.[5]

In contrast to Newton's notion of the world as a giant pendulum clock, with its planets timelessly orbiting, these nineteenth-century scientists viewed the world as a giant machine, one which was running down, losing energy, becoming increasingly disorganized, and tending toward ever greater homogeneity and eventual heat death.[6] Those involved in the study of thermodynamics distinguished between reversible processes (independent of time) and irreversible processes (dependent on the direction of time); they tended, however, to be more interested in the study of reversible processes, with the irreversible ones viewed as nuisances not worthy of study.[7] What is fundamental for our purposes, however, is that classical science had been challenged by the central issue of time—or by what Arthur Stanley Eddington called "time's arrow . . . this one-way property of time which has no analogue in space."[8] Time moves only in one direction; events cannot be reproduced as they had been in the past; systems are no longer reproducible, because time invariably transforms them.[9]

Indeed, the nineteenth century may well be regarded as the century in which time began to be important in numerous fields—those of astronomy, biology, geology, social evolution, and language, for example.[10] Darwin's concept of evolution incorporated the notion of irreversible time within it. Living organisms developed through time from simpler to more complex ones, from undifferentiated forms to differentiated ones. In the development of a species, time is irreversible: a more complex form will not return to its simpler state, but will evolve into something new. Thus, a second nineteenth century science, that of evolutionary biology, integrated the concept of time within its theoretical foundations.

While both biologists and physicists recognized the centrality of time to their studies of order, there was also a fundamental difference in their notions of change. For the thermodynamicists, the effect of time was to break natural processes down into more and more dissipative structures, leading eventually to equilibrium as energy became evenly distributed as heat. For the followers of Darwin, biological

systems were becoming more and more complex and differentiated, leading to greater organization within the individual system. Could both of them be right? Which principle of irreversible time held greater universality? Can we
determine the effect of time, and attempt to understand its
processes? Is time absolute or relative to experience? Commonly, we confuse time with its representations. Time is not
a river and it cannot flow except in metaphor. Nor is it the
motion in space of a clock and clocks do not really tell the
time. Furthermore, the time, space, and motion of clocks
are not absolute.

Quite without intending to undermine Newtonian mechanics—which assumed the reality of absolute space, time
and measurement, and therefore of a completely predictable
universe—twentieth century physicists nevertheless did so by
creating the hypotheses of relativity and quantum mechanics. While Einstein began with the conviction that the universe was timeless and had a fundamentally simple structure—a position he tried to save by denying that quantum
mechanics was anything more than makeshift—his own work
implied a universe of great complexity and with characteristics he did not accept. He proposed the hypothesis that if
light were thought of as having a constant speed for all
observers, regardless of their position and momentum, then
each observer would necessarily have a unique measure of
time and each would be different from all the others. By this
hypothesis, called the theory of general relativity and so far
consistently supported by experiment, Einstein destroyed
the idea of absolute time—a linear time-scale measured as
identical by any observer—on which Newtonian mechanics
depended. With relativity, each observer has a personal
measure of time that depends on position and momentum,
whether the clock be electronic, mechanical or biological.
As the physicist, Stephen Hawking puts it:

Before 1915, space and time were thought of as a fixed arena in which events took place, but which was not affected by what happened in it . . . It was natural to think that space and time went on forever. . . . [However] space and time are now dynamic quantities: when a body moves, or a force acts, it affects the curvature of space and time—and in turn the structure of space-time affects the way in which bodies move and forces act. Space and time not only affect but also are affected by everything that happens in the universe . . . The old idea of an essentially unchanging universe that could have existed, and could continue to exist, forever was replaced by the notion of a dynamic, expanding universe that seemed to have begun a finite time ago, and might end at a finite time in the future. . . . And years later . . . Roger Penrose and I showed that Einstein's general theory of relativity implied that the universe must have a beginning and, possibly, an end.[11]

Convinced by the successes of science as he perceived them in the early nineteenth century, the French physicist, the Marquis de LaPlace had asserted that there existed a set of discoverable physical laws which would explain anything that happened. He believed that if we could, like God, establish completely the state of the universe at one time, we could use Newtonian mechanics to calculate its state at any other time in the future or the past. By 1900, resistance to this idea among scientists was supported by a number of outcomes of the application of Newton's laws which blatantly contradicted experimental observation. The German physicist, Max Planck, suggested the quantum hypothesis as a way of saving the Newtonian synthesis. It viewed light, X-rays, radio and other waves as packets of particles called quanta with characteristics which agreed with the results of observation. In 1926, Werner Heisenberg pointed out that a necessary outcome of the quantum hypothesis was what is called the uncertainty principle—the inability to determine the position of a given particle, because the act of measuring disturbed the velocity of the particle being measured, whatever the means of measurement. The more accurate the measuring attempt, the more the particle was disturbed. Heisenberg also showed that this uncertainty was a fundamental, inescapable property of the physical universe.

This unexpected outcome of the quantum hypothesis put an end to the LaPlace vision of a completely determined universe and replaced absolute Newtonian mechanics with a quantum mechanics founded on an inescapable randomness which affected the physical sciences at every level except, so far, the large-scale structures involving gravity.

Quantum mechanics also involves the observing subject inescapably in the act of measuring the observed object, an outcome which destroyed the dream of objective science, whose essence was that it could have no effect on the universe "out there" because that universe did not depend in any way on the subjective intentions of scientists or other inquirers.[12]

Together, the theory of relativity and the principle of uncertainty and its corollary, complementarity, mean that neither an absolute nor a predictable physical universe is possible, that no phenomenon is real unless it is observed, that human intentions affect the structure of the physical world and that it is impossible to find a single theoretical language to describe all the variables in any physical system. These statements constitute a complete denial of the absolutes of the Newtonian universe.

Such matters may seem distant from the day-to-day activity of historians, but they are not. Historians, like the rest of college-educated professionals, have been deeply influenced by the Newtonian perception of things, especially by the idea of absolute time underlying the modern sense of historical chronology which places events on an absolute linear time-scale. For example, comparative history of any kind, in its current form, depends on the ability to place widely divergent facts on a single time-line. Relativity and uncertainty do challenge the way history is done and the challenge is not simply philosophical, because the assumption of absolute time excludes a large part of human experience from historical inquiry. Any events not precisely located in time, such as thinking, growth, attitudes, cultural assumptions, or the meaning of artifacts, are excluded from present historical practice, except on *ad hoc* grounds.

The challenge to objectivity inherent in the history of the scientific ideas described here is thoroughgoing and undeniable and historians, like other inquirers, must face the consequences of admitting that they are part of the world they describe and analyze.[13]

Philosophers and social theorists of the post–World War II era have begun to deal with the implications of the findings of scientists. In 1962, the historian, Thomas Kuhn, published *The Structure of Scientific Revolutions*, a book which has become a basic reference point for discussions on the nature of scientific knowledge.[14] Distinguishing between three stages of scientific knowledge (the preparadigmatic, dominant, and extraordinary), Kuhn argues that the *process* of scientific inquiry is fundamentally similar to the research process of *any* inquiry; science has no unique methodology that is both completely objective and universally valid. The researchers are themselves part of the process of inquiry, and therefore the presuppositions of those researchers' culture enter into the process itself. There is no possibility of a divorce between subjective and objective reality.[15]

In the same year that Kuhn published his work, the philosopher Karl Popper also rejected the notion that there could be absolute knowledge in *any* discipline:

> The way in which knowledge progresses, and especially our scientific knowledge, is by unjustified (and unjustifiable) anticipations, by guesses, by tentative solutions to our problems, by *conjectures*.[16]

Scientific knowledge, according to Popper, was nothing else but "... the growth of ordinary human knowledge *writ large*...."[17] While he did acknowledge that we have in science a good "criterion of progress"[18] which enables us to learn from our mistakes more clearly than in social experiences, his fundamental premise is that all human knowledge is fallible and transitory.

Building upon the mind-set that made the work of Kuhn and Popper possible, a group of "post-empiricist" philosophers[19] is altering our notion of the nature of rationality in scientific inquiry. Such thinkers as Hans-Georg Gadamer, Jürgen Habermas, Richard Rorty, Jacques Derrida, and Michel Foucault "... delineate a type of rationality that is historically situated and practical, involving choice, deliberation, and judgement."[20] In an attempt to move beyond the questions posed by Descartes and the philosophy of logical positivism, contemporary philosophers are redefining the notions of reason, knowledge, and truth. As Bernstein writes of Gadamer:

> ... he rejects the oppositions that have been so entrenched since the Enlightenment—between reason and tradition, reason and prejudice, reason and authority. Reason is not a faculty or capacity that can free itself from its historical context and horizons. Reason is historical or situated reason which gains its distinctive power always within a living tradition.[21]

Such thinking challenges the very framework for the distinctions between "hard" and "soft" sciences, or between scientific and humanistic modes of inquiry.

During the last two decades a third and equally controversial wave of innovation in physics has arrived called "chaos." Unlike particle physics which is involved with "micro-events" far distant from human experience, chaos is concerned with the "macro-event" scale of everyday human life. Its grand question is how, in a universe governed by the

Second Law of Thermodynamics and moving relentlessly toward greater and greater disorder, does order arise? How does order come out of chaos?

Chaos as a program of inquiry had one of its major origins in the scientific backwater of meteorology where turbulence and coherence, unpredictability and pattern exist simultaneously. The weather, like history, is a mixed, complex world in which similar events succeed themselves differently. In a well-known metaphor called the Butterfly Effect, the meteorologist, Edward Lorenz, described a butterfly flitting through the air in Peking whose movements soon influenced storm systems in New York. The idea underlying the image is that very small differences can rapidly create large-scale effects—that the physical world we recognize is characterized by extremely sensitive dependence on initial conditions, so that tiny changes in particular elements of a system could lead to large and incalculable changes in overall behavior. Lorenz discovered that quite simple nonlinear mathematical equations could model turbulent systems because they, too, behaved unpredictably, but at the time exhibited internal patterns, just like the weather. Other scientists found the same juxtaposition of order and chaos in other phenomena, such as the heartbeat, dripping faucets, the formation of crystals, the immune system, economic systems, earthquakes, population dynamics, and the operation of memory.

A mathematician, Benoit Mandelbrot, and a physicist, Mitchell J. Feigenbaum, became interested in different ways in recursive patterns. Mandelbrot's *fractals* are an expression of those kinds of patterns which are self-similar or self-referential at smaller and smaller scales. The fractal repeats the same mathematical transformation at smaller and smaller dimensions so that, even under immense magnification, its self-embedded pattern is recognizable. Feigenbaum's special notion of universality was applied to recursive patterns in different physical systems which appeared disorderly and chaotic. He claimed that all physical systems behave measurably in the same self-referential manner at the point of transition between orderliness and turbulence and that such behavior is what happens in systems when they work on themselves recursively again and again.

The universe pictured by this new physics is one in which chaos in time recursively creates order, in which randomness with direction evolves into orderly complexity and in which dissipation of energy is a generator of order.[22]

THE POST-POSITIVIST MODEL FROM SCIENCE: PRIGOGINE

While philosophers and philosophers of science have understood the need to rethink the dichotomies that have existed since the time of Aristotle, or at least since the time of Descartes, few scientists have tried to apply this "post-empiricist" mentality to the discipline of science. In 1977, however, a radically new conceptualization of science was presented by Ilya Prigogine, who won the Nobel Prize in chemistry for his study of "dissipative structures"—structures which are far from equilibrium, and which can be transformed from disorder (chaos) into new order. But Prigogine was also interested in understanding the connections between biology and physics and, together with Isabelle Stengers, wrote an extraordinarily suggestive work, *Order Out of Chaos*. In this work, they present a radically altered view of science, one which compels us ". . . to reexamine its goals, its methods, its epistemology."[23] For historians, this work has great significance because it rests on the model of history itself. In his study of the relationship of the microscopic to the macroscopic, Prigogine contends that the history of civilization provides the insight for understanding science.[24]

History provides this understanding because of its *integration of time into nature*. That concept of time enables Prigogine to demonstrate the relationship between entropy and evolution, and thereby to develop a new epistemology for science. That he has used the model of history to do so turns the age-old effort to justify history amongst the social sciences on its head. History, properly understood, provides the model for science, because of its very concern with the categories of time and human experience.

Of critical importance to Prigogine is the concept of irreversibility, a concept which incorporates the temporal and gives nature its direction. In grappling with the question of whether that direction is evolutionary or entropic, Prigogine developed his concept of dissipative structures. Such structures function as open systems and can utilize environmental resources which help them to maintain their internal order; this, in turn, means that such structures are capable of evolving into higher, more complex forms. But open systems also lead to greater entropy. The direction they go in is a function of time and chance. Dissipative structures evolve when random motions (therefore unpredictable ones) of microscopic particles produce phase changes. Significant changes are possible because at this microscopic level, the particles are free, permitting the occurrence of unique events. Thus, scientific nature both moves and changes. When a system reaches a point which is more complex than its own organizational capabilities, it reaches bifurcation points, in which a system can reorder itself, leading to new stability. It is the interaction of the external and internal which leads to such bifurcation points and to the ability to endure catastrophe. As Robert Artigiani has written, "Continuity and discontinuity, order and transition succeed each other in ways which can never be predicted."[25]

Prigogine's paradigm can be contrasted with the classical dynamics paradigm in a number of ways: (1) It is qualitative

in nature, treating change qualitatively rather than quanti-
tatively; (2) It is time-oriented, recognizing that the universe
as a whole is far from a state of equilibrium, and therefore
must be viewed as an irreversible system; (3) The observer
is also time-oriented, and therefore there is no value-free or
value-neutral science. Rather, subject and object interact in
a connected process.

History and the process of time are central to Prigogine's
epistemology. To date, historians have failed to recognize
the implications for their own discipline. Let us, therefore,
illustrate the connections between science and history even
more directly. Prigogine postulates that the introduction of
the concept of history will integrate time into the scientific
picture of nature and thereby complete it. History requires
that time really pass and that structures actually evolve. History as well creates a picture of nature as a self-contained
system which includes both ourselves and the external world
as necessary to each other. Objectivity becomes only one of
a number of perspectives necessary to know nature. This
historical science proposed by Prigogine perceives a temporal and irreversibly changing nature in which the past
conditions the future and entropy and evolution are treated
as complementary processes. In such a science, life is not
Monod's impossible alien; it is the unexpected outcome of
evolutionary changes, one of which is the human intelligence
which creates knowledge out of its own evolved nature. In
the evolutionary paradigm, knowledge is simultaneously objective and participatory. The strained attempts so many historians have made to be "objective" have been based on a
misconception of scientific "truth." Scientists, too, are
slowly ridding themselves of a conception of an objective
reality that requires the denial of novelty, diversity and value
in the name of immutable laws. Prigogine maintains that
scientists

... have rid themselves of a fascination with a rationality taken as
closed and a knowledge seen as nearly achieved. They are now open
to the unexpected, which they no longer define as the result of
imperfect knowledge or insufficient control.[26]

This radical shift in perspective—a change prefigured by Diderot, Poincaré, Charles Peirce, Darwin, Maxwell, Whitehead and others—toward the temporal, complex, ambiguous, multiple and many-layered world of the historian—brings scientists and humanists together to share and pursue an integrated epistemology of nature and world order. The two-century old conflict between scientist and humanist is no longer substantial.

This opening up of science to concerns often termed humanistic, but now again obviously universal, has some immediate implications for the discipline of history. One effect is to rehabilitate the importance of generalization as a useful and legitimate aspect of methodology. A second is to show that it is altogether reasonable to treat causation cautiously as a complex issue. A third is to justify the use of significance as a principle of selection. The most obvious, of course, is to make time once more a central dimension in the creation of knowledge. From this perspective, many aspects of historical method previously rejected by the so-called "hard" social sciences now begin to exhibit a depth of meaning. In short, the epistemology proposed by Prigogine ironically provides the new scientific basis for a methodology of history, because it is now clear that history is a human science which does furnish knowledge of consequences to people concerned with practical outcomes. History supplies knowledge which can be used in the world of affairs.

THE COMPLEMENTARITY OF SCIENTIFIC AND HISTORICAL MODELS: BRAUDEL

Like all epistemologies, Prigogine's analysis of science focuses on the *process* for obtaining knowledge rather than the *product* of knowledge. In this process, he argues, scientists must consider the impact of time as an agent of change, the potential for unpredictable developments which create new structures, and the inevitable effect of the observer on that which is observed. For Prigogine, history provides examples of social systems which clearly illustrate and therefore validate the above processes. We can take this analysis a step further, and demonstrate how a leading historian has already developed a similar world view. Such efforts become especially interesting in the light of Prigogine's work, because they establish models for reconstituting the discipline of history.

One internationally renowned historian who has insisted that history must be written to reveal world order is Fernand Braudel. His massive, two-volume work, *La Mediterraneé*, was first published in 1949, revised in 1966, and translated into English in 1972. It reflects an effort to explore the whole Mediterranean world and to create a work of synthesis, demonstrating the fundamental unity, coherence, and greatness of the Mediterranean region.[27] This vast undertaking begins with the geophysical world, as Braudel explores the role of the environment—its peninsulas composed of mountains, plateaus, and plains; its seas and coasts; its boundaries with Africa, Europe, and the Atlantic; its climate; its communication networks by land and sea. This is one of the voices of the history of the Mediterranean, the voice of a history ". . . whose passage is almost imperceptible, . . . a history in which all change is slow, a history of constant repetition, ever-recurring cycles."[28] This macroscopic geophysical world is, for Braudel, the "constant" of the Mediterranean; these "unspectacular structures" are nonetheless the underlying reference grid for all else that follows.[29] In Prigogine's terminology, this is the world in equilibrium, or near-equilibrium. It is the world which can be structurally dissected, as

Braudel does in the first 352 pages of his English edition, to reveal the predictable, the recurrent, and the near time-less. But even this study of geographical space must have some larger value, or the structure itself is meaningless. For Braudel, " . . . all the evidence combines across time and space, to give us a history in slow motion from which per-manent values can be detected."[30]

The second part of his book, called "Collective Destinies and General Trends," explores the economic and social structures of the Mediterranean, tackling the ". . . economic systems, states, societies, civilizations, the indispensable in-struments of exchange, and lastly the different forms of war."[31] While, according to Braudel, this takes us closer to the individual, it continues to explore a long-term perspec-tive, thereby combining structure and conjuncture, ". . . the permanent and the ephemeral," which constantly integrates that which endures and that which changes.[32] For Prigogine, such an analysis would demonstrate the rate of entropy pro-duction, discovering the necessary relationship between that which proceeds towards more and more complex systems in an evolutionary process and that which dissipates and loses energy. One could also thereby explore the emergence of new systems from the old (the bifurcation points), the cre-ation of new forms of order from that which has become disorderly, or chaotic. The social and economic structures are open systems, which can utilize environmental resources to help them maintain their internal order. They are struc-tures which are capable of evolving into higher, more com-plex forms, but which also simultaneously lead toward greater entropy.[33] Analysis at this level, Braudel cautions, is neither infallible nor capable of providing total undisputed truth. It leads to useful formulations of problems, not ul-timate resolutions of issues.[34] As Braudel looks at this di-mension of time—a dimension of slow but perceptible rhythms, he perceives the decline of material existence, a growing decadence and malfunctioning of its vital sectors.[35] Refusing to fall victim to a simplistic theory of inevitable decay, or to a law or irreversible decline, he insists that the Mediterranean has its own structure, and must be studied in its temporal as well as its spatial context. And in its unique space, that Mediterranean world was fundamentally one of peasants, tenant farmers, and landowners, dependent on harvests:

> Peasants and crops, in other words food supplies and the size of
> the population, silently determined the destiny of the age. In both
> the long and the short term, agricultural life was all-important.[36]

The study of the Mediterranean world illustrates the effect of the grain crises in the 1580s. Such grain crises, although short term, specific "events," are part of the structural geo-political reality of this world order. Thus, the microscopic and macroscopic, the predictable and the chance events, interacted to create a slow decline, a loss of "heat" or "energy," which in time would lead to a new historical reality with the end of Mediterranean predominance. The civilization of the Mediterranean world, like all other civilizations, is a dissipative structure which arranges matter, energy, and human behavior in a particular way. It is an example of "negative entropy," which is designed to perpetuate effective behavioral patterns.[37]

There is still a third section to Braudel's book, termed "Events, Politics, and People." For Braudel, this is traditional history, written on the scale of individual men, looking at the ". . . brief, rapid, nervous fluctuations," as he explores "micro-history." In addition to the Olympian view which preceded, one must also explore the "ephemeral." Braudel clearly distrusts this Rankean form of history, in which time is extremely short term, and in which individual actions are given weight beyond their significance in perspective. At the same time, if a total history is to be written, this is the part which is most passionate, most exciting, and richest in human interest. It is, then, one of the planes upon which history must be explored—the plane of individual time.[38] As Braudel traces the individual wars, the development of the Holy League, the Turco-Spanish treaties, and the personality of Philip II, he is not at all sure of the meaning of such events in the scheme of total history. For although these individuals represent the free particles of the natural universe, they may not, in fact, be so free as they believe they are. Their freedom is limited by the circumstances of geophysical and socio-economic space. As Braudel concludes:

> So when I think of the individual, I am always inclined to see him imprisoned within a destiny in which he himself has little hand, fixed in a landscape in which the infinite perspectives of the long term stretch into the distance both behind him and before. In historical analysis as I see it, rightly or wrongly, the long run always wins in the end. Annihilating innumerable events . . . it indubitably limits both the freedom of the individual and even the role of chance. I am by temperament a 'structuralist', little tempted by the event, or even by the short-term conjuncture which is after all merely a grouping of events in the same area. But the historian's 'structuralism' . . . does not tend towards the mathematical abstraction of relations expressed as functions, but instead towards the very sources of life in its most concrete, everyday, indestructible and anonymously human expression.[39]

In this last sentence Braudel hints at the point made by the students of chaos, like Prigogine, who have shown—in a way similar to the "Butterfly Effect" in meteorology—that the consequences of a single, anonymous human act over a long period can transform an entire civilization. Like evolutionary change in biology, this transformation cannot be foreseen, but it can be accounted for, sometimes with great difficulty, in retrospect, because qualitatively similar patterns recognizably reoccur. Historians know this frustrating "re-peatability" intuitively but have been unable to deal with it theoretically. Chaos theory appears to provide the basis for understanding both the repetition of patterns and their un-predictability. Braudel's approach provides the larger con-text of regularity in which the changes occur.

Thus, for Braudel in history, as for Prigogine in science, the aim of any study is to deal with complexity. Fundamen-tally, Braudel sees the world of men in much the same terms as Prigogine sees the world of things. Civilizations are dis-sipative structures which organize biological and other forms of matter and energy, establishing limitations as a result of their own mechanisms. Culture is to human society as the template molecule is to scientific order: it controls and di-rects, creating values which in turn serve to perpetuate ex-isting structures.[40] For both, there is no single controlling order, but rather a process of change and development. For Prigogine, there are microscopic and macroscopic struc-tures, some determined, some random. The observer, also, affects the physical reality he observes. Similarly, Braudel recognizes that his study of the Mediterranean world is not a totally objective dissection of its individualized parts. It arose out of his "passion" for the region; and his view of the region changed as a result of specialized research gen-erated by his initial study and his own growth between the first and second editions. That growth, he acknowledges, led him to perceive the entire work differently, reconsidering the dialectic of space and time to place more emphasis on economics, political science, and civilization.[41]

Ultimately, then, history for Braudel is ". . . a song for many voices," a perspective rather than a narrative of events, a constantly evolving process between observer and ob-served, and necessarily a human endeavor.[42] It is not, strictly speaking, an exclusively inventive venture, because it is based on the reality of past evidence, where it can be found.[43] For the scientist, nature's real obstinacy acts as a test of theories. Similarly, for the historian, the reality of past evidence limits the acceptability of generalizations. Even this evidence, for both historian and scientist, is not complete or final, because it is collected by people whose vision is culturally limited; it is selective on two levels.[44] Despite such caveats, Braudel has composed a monumental work which has had few critics during its almost two decades in print. In the 1980s, we can recognize it as a work which conforms to the latest findings by scientists. It is not just a history, but a philosophy and a methodology thoroughly consistent with modern scientific concepts of universal order.

A HISTORICAL METHODOLOGY FOR PUBLIC AND ACADEMIC HISTORY

This shared epistemology and methodology of Braudel and Prigogine affirm the common process for rational inquiry.[45] Implicit in their epistemology is the belief that inquiry is a process in which the observer and observed are inseparable, and in which there is a fluid, interactive relationship between any hypothesis and its test. While Prigogine provides an epistemology, and Braudel offers a methodological model, neither directly discusses the basic process which is required to bring a historical investigation to fruition. This process, which includes research, analysis, expression, and presentation, is the foundation upon which the discipline of history and all historical work rests. It is, however, too often left to the individual historian to discover the relationship of these processes to a basic methodology. Now that we have determined that scientific and historical inquiry properly understood are essentially the same, it is important to discuss these processes in some detail.

RESEARCH: From the time of Ranke, there has been an assumption that the historian *should* begin his investigation with empirical "facts" which will, in time, lead to theories or generalizations. The facts, it was believed, would speak for themselves; the role of the historian was to collect these facts while standing apart from them, and then when he had completed his collection, he should categorize those facts and ultimately write a fully objective analysis of their meaning.

We now know that such claims of objectivity are not possible for any science, and do not lead to better understanding. Historians, like scientists, build on interpretations which precede their investigation. Secondary sources (or previous research on a specific or related topic) form a cultural perspective; primary sources generate unexpectedly different and often revolutionizing ways of understanding past events. What is fundamental for the historical process is that historians develop as clear an understanding as possible of the complex interrelationships that exist between sources of whatever kind and their interpretation. This understanding begins with collecting and initial categorizing of materials. Simply placing some material in one category and other material in another will establish primitive interpretive patterns which are likely to influence how the researcher proceeds to examine the records of the past. As research progresses, the historian must maintain an awareness of the dialectical relationship between sources and their interpretation and the necessary part the judgments of the researcher play in the process.

The historian, then, conducts his research into the past record in much the same way that the scientist carries out his research into physical structures. There can be no testing of every hypothesis; often theories in the physical sciences are presented before verification and can never *in principle* be completely verified. But theories allow for predictions and inferences which are subject to tests. Hypotheses, then, allow the investigation of causal relationships which utilize new data and new factors. Such hypotheses enlarge the investigator's intellectual universe, and ultimately provide a basis for the kinds of insights that lead to conjectural syntheses. Negative correlations can be as useful in advancing knowledge as positive ones.[46] As the historians continue to select their materials, they must recognize that they exercise judgments of value in organizing, categorizing, and even in collecting their evidence. Historians interact with their facts in this process, being affected both by previous interpretations, by their own *values*, by their place in *time*, and by their discoveries of data along the way. As Winthrop Jordan has written, ". . . an historian's relationship with the raw materials of history is a profoundly reciprocal one. . . ."[47]

Because so many historians have accepted the assumption that the historian's search into the past could be fully objective—an assumption found to be untrue for any inquiry—they have severely limited themselves in terms of utilizable sources. It is here that the academic historian can profit from the knowledge attained by public historians, who often must make sense of a diversity of sketchy materials. These public historians, presented with such evidence as kitchen artifacts, war memorabilia, clothing, annual reports, and orally expressed memories, must reconstruct a picture of the past from highly selective data, frequently reflecting an individual's concerns or the concerns of a narrowly defined community seeking its own glorification. Despite Braudel's statement that the individual is often the least important basis from which to measure meaningful change, such evidence must be employed by the historian. By using both artifactual and oral evidence as significant sources, the historian can weigh the relationship between the general and the specific. The public historian often begins with data from the individual perspective, while the academic historian begins with data representing finite conclusions about a society developed by itself. Greater interaction among these different sources will lead to a better understanding of the relationship between microscopic and macroscopic events within a defined civilization, and may also lead to surprising, creative insights into group consciousness, human psychology, and continuities and discontinuities within societies. The more diverse the sources, the more complex the interrelationships, the more interdisciplinary the theories, the more productive the results can be.

Those public historians who maintain our national and local past through museums, historic homes, and site preservation, should well understand the research challenges faced by those who study preliterate cultures. In many ways, African history is similar in its elements to public history. Jan Vansina, in his *Kingdoms of the Savanna*, was a pioneer in developing techniques for using oral traditions as dependable sources. As well, he used material culture sources, linguistics, archaeology, anthropology, sociology, economics, and, of course, Portuguese and other European documentary sources.[48] The written sources, while important and necessary, were but a part of Vansina's historical inquiry conceived as a unified process. His use of sources to analyze an otherwise "lost" culture conforms with the advice given by Febvre, that the historian must be a geographer, linguist, sociologist, psychologist, and must utilize any other discipline which will help him to reveal "total history."[49] While few academic historians today would quarrel with the incorporation of theory from other "social-scientific" disciplines, many continue to scorn the importance of historical research that uses "undependable" sources to study "unimportant" subject matter with a "lowly" status. Such elitists continue to exhibit the view expressed by Hugh Trevor-Roper in 1965, who proclaimed history as a bastion of high civilization. He argued then, three years before the publication of Vansina's book, that there could be no history of black Africa, because the only evidence that existed was that of Europeans in Africa. "The rest," he wrote:

> is largely darkness, like the history of pre-European, pre-Columbian America. And darkness is not a subject for history.[50]

Such a view of sources within the discipline of history reflects a myopic vision of the possibilities for historical research. Public historians have demonstrated that the incorporation of three diverse kinds of sources—oral, material culture, and documentary—and the absorption of skills, techniques, and methods from related disciplines, can greatly enrich the understanding of a cultural heritage. Unfortunately, it remains for the academic historians to learn from the lessons of our colleagues in public history, and to integrate this greater complexity into their own teaching and research methodologies. To do so would be consistent with the Braudel/Prigogine model for rational inquiry.

ANALYSIS: It should be clear that research and analysis are interrelated processes for the historian. Research must begin from some framework, which itself suggests some initial formulation of a hypothesis or theory by the historian. As research proceeds, historians analyze their data on many different levels. They must simultaneously gather the "facts" and interpret them. As they evaluate the meaning of the facts, they are led to new sources, which are chosen on the basis of some judgment (or analysis) by the historians themselves. Thus, there can be no research in isolation of analysis and judgments of value.

As Prigogine and Braudel understand, historians and scientists enrich their analysis by incorporating a multiplicity of perspectives. They must look both at qualitative and quantitative indicators of change. They must, in other words, be able to recognize when a movement (e.g., an ideology) or a development (e.g., industrialization) or a technical innovation (e.g., contraceptive devices) becomes so large in scale that it reflects a qualitative change in the nature of the community, society, or culture under study. In Prigogine's terms, they must be able to determine whether or not such developments represent "bifurcation points" which lead to new organizations of the human environment. Furthermore, historians must analyze data in terms which support the regularity of events or their randomness. In their analyses, they should be able to demonstrate what accounts for change. In so doing, they must explore the geophysical factors, sociocultural factors, and unique technological, biographical, or accidental elements which affect their examinations. They must be able to distinguish repetitive and nonrepetitive patterns. They must recognize that historical interpreters are themselves products of their environments, stand along the continuum of time, and are fundamentally shaped by time. In short, historians must be able to generalize, to establish significance, to illustrate the role of time, and to demonstrate the multicausal, complex, and multiple nature of the past and its relationship to the present. As E. H. Carr has written:

> History is concerned with the relation between the unique and the general. As a historian, you can no more separate them, or give precedence to one over the other, than you can separate fact and interpretation.[51]

The obligation of intelligent analysis is critical to the discipline of history. Without such analysis, history is merely the chronicling of past events.

These aspects of analysis are equally relevant for the public and the academic historian. Frequently, public historians are given a narrowly defined task and a time limit, and asked to come up with a useful interpretation. Whether it be in the history of a corporation, in the annual report of a governmental agency, in the exhibit of Civil War artifacts, in the display of cookery and recipes of a bygone era, or in the policy analysis of legislative intent, public historians must present their findings in some meaningful framework. Their tasks are often constrained by the nature of documentation available and by the budget and time limitations of their clients. Their analyses will therefore be more or less meaningful because of the depth of their own historical knowledge. Public historians' understanding of history and in particular, their awareness of the analytical process, will determine whether they succeed or fail at their tasks. They often are asked to focus on the particular; this skill will be demonstrated by their ability to put the particular into a more general context, and to explicate the relationship between the general and the unique.

Likewise, academic historians face a similar problem, although one over which they have greater control, for academic historians define their own research endeavor for the most part. The conventions of the academy have led many historians to continue to examine history "from the top." Indeed, those who have broken out of this realm—the social, ethnic, and women's historians—are frequently those who best understand the potential for public history. Traditional academic historians often cull the documents to explain trends—in political behavior, diplomatic relations, demography, or ideas—but all too often are unable to incorporate the particular or chance or unique events which give dimension, as Braudel writes, to the ". . . anger, dreams, or illusions" of men.[52]

What is needed is a fundamental reconstitution of the discipline of history. For historians to function as meaningful analysts, they must try to create a complete discipline. For that endeavor to succeed, the approaches of the public historian and academic historian must be combined. Only then can historians claim to have a methodological approach which establishes them as expert analysts of societies and civilizations.

EXPRESSION AND PRESENTATION: All historians must decide upon a mode of expression for their findings. Again, historians have been largely unwilling to explore the multiplicity of models available for expressing research findings. A mode of presentation—a format—often is chosen in conjunction with goals, materials, and audience. Such a decision is itself an analytic one. The process of editing sources, for example, is both technical and theoretical. It is technical in the sense that expression must be correct. To this end, editorial skills require familiarity with usages of spelling, grammar, diction, mechanics, and other aspects of language. In addition, however, an editor must decide on a style which best represents the information to be presented and the audience to be reached. Finally, there is a far more subtle process of editing in which format and language combine to best represent the author's focus and to best demonstrate the underlying historical processes. Historians must decide not only which materials are most important to support their analyses, but must edit their materials for the correctness, structure, content, and integrity of both subject and process.

Determining a mode of expression is but one step towards deciding upon a mode of presentation. The two are linked fundamentally as part of the process used by all historians in their efforts to market their findings most effectively. These presentations can take a multiplicity of forms: examples include museum exhibits, marketing reports, policy analyses, brochures, journals, books, films, and tapes. At the most fundamental level, the mode of presentation is related to the audience to be reached. Presentation of findings will accomplish nothing if there is no audience. Thus, historians must consciously determine a marketing strategy. Their research, analysis, and expression are necessarily connected with an already established notion of audience. Their findings should not differ to please a particular audience, but their modes of presentation most surely will.

It is in the final productions of the historical process that public and academic historians differ most markedly. Academic historians frequently define their audience narrowly: they usually write for each other. Writing within a "professional" mode for which they have been trained through research and writing seminars, they tend to scorn any suggestion of marketing their works. The value of academic historians' work is judged primarily by other historians, rather than by the public.

Public historians, however, attempt to determine their audiences self-consciously. Their success is often measured by their ability to have an impact on the wider public, particularly if they are engaged in cultural resource management or policy analysis. Thus public historians, unlike their academic counterparts, must understand how to make practical decisions about funds, numbers, politics, interagency conflicts, and other aspects of the world of affairs. Public historians work far more within the constraints established by others than do academic historians. At the same time, however, public historians may have greater opportunities to develop a particular public's self-consciousness and understanding and therefore to initiate social change. With such potential, public historians must take very seriously their professional responsibility to present the past with integrity, for while academic historians are responsible mainly to their peers, public historians have their primary responsibility to the wider public whose understanding of their world they have influenced.

Public and academic historians should not be viewed as pursuing two distinct "tracks" which require different kinds of training programs. Historians of whatever stamp share a common methodology and common processes. Fundamental to their endeavor is the focus on research and analysis. This research and analysis, moreover, is no different in its essential character in science than in history. Thus, as historians seek to sell their skills in the marketplace, they must understand that it is precisely their unique ability to deal with time and with human experience that provides them with their analytic strengths. Rather than apologizing for their failure to successfully emulate social scientists, they should recognize that social scientific techniques, still largely based on Newtonian dynamics and rigidly reductionist principles, are now inadequate. The methodology and techniques of history are once more a part of the mainstream of a more universal science of inquiry.

NOTES

1. Richard Bernstein, *Beyond Objectivism and Relativism: Science, Hermenentics, and Praxis* (Philadelphia: University of Pennsylvania Press, 1985).
2. Jacques Monod, *Chance and Necessity* (New York: Vintage Books, 1972), 172–173.
3. Ilya Prigogine and Isabelle Stenger, *Order Out of Chaos: Man's New Dialogue With Nature* (New York: Bantam Books, 1984), 294.
4. *Ibid.*, 12.
5. *Ibid.*, 117. See also *Unabridged Dictionary of the English Language* (N.Y.: Randam House, 1967).
6. Prigogine, *Order Out of Chaos*, xiii–xiv; 12, 103–118.
7. *Ibid.*, 12.
8. Arthur Stanley Eddington, *The Nature of the Physical World* (New York: The Macmillan Company, 1928), 66–67, 69.
9. Prigogine, *Order Out of Chaos*, xix–xx.
10. *Ibid.*, 116.

11. Stephen W. Hawking, *A Brief History of Time From the Big Bang to Black Holes* (New York: Bantam, 1988), pp. 33–34.
12. Heinz R. Pagels, *The Cosmic Code: Quantum Physics As The Language of Nature* (New York: Bantam, 1983), 67–81.
13. Donald J. Wilcox, *The Measures of Times Past: Pre-Newtonian Chronologies and the Rhetoric of Relative Time* (Chicago: The University of Chicago Press, 1987) 39–50.
14. Quentin Skinner, ed., *The Return of Grand Theory in the Human Sciences* (New York: Cambridge University Press, 1985), 85.
15. *Ibid.*, 85–92; Bernstein, *Beyond Objectivism and Relativism*, 21–23. Thomas Kuhn, *The Structure of Scientific Revolutions* (Chicago: University of Chicago Press, 1962), 1–9.
16. Karl R. Popper, *Conjectures and Refutations: The Growth of Scientific Knowledge* (New York: Basic Books, 1962), Preface, vii.
17. *Ibid.*, 216.
18. Karl Popper, "Some Comments on Truth and the Growth of Knowledge," in Ernest Nagel, Patrick Suppes, and Alfred Tarski, *Logic, Methodology and Philosophy of Science* (California: Stanford University Press, 1962), 285.
19. Bernstein, *Beyond Objectivism and Relativism*, 20.
20. *Ibid.*, xiv. See also Skinner, ed., *The Return of Grand Theory*.
21. Bernstein, *Beyond Objectivism and Relativism*, 37.
22. James Gleick, *Chaos: Making a New Science* (New York: Viking, Penguin, Inc., 1987), 5–8, 83–118, 157–187, 303–317.
23. Prigogine, *Order Out of Chaos*, Introduction by Alvin Toffler, xii.
24. *Ibid.*, 191–192.
25. We are indebted to Robert Artigiani for this synthesis of Prigogine's thesis, which is incorporated into an unpublished paper, entitled "Thermodynamics and History: Using Prigogine's Dissipative Structures to Produce a Philosophy of History."
26. Prigogine, *Order Out of Chaos*, 306.
27. Fernand Braudel, *The Mediterranean and the Mediterranean World in the Age of Philip II*, trans. Sian Reynolds (2 vols., New York: Harper and Row, 1972), 14.
28. *Ibid.*, Vol. I, 20.
29. *Ibid.*, Vol. II, 1239.
30. *Ibid.*, Vol. I, 23.
31. *Ibid.*, 353.
32. *Ibid.*
33. See above, p. 66.

34. Braudel, *The Mediterranean*, Vol. I, 899.
35. *Ibid.*, Vol. II, 1240.
36. *Ibid.*, 1241.
37. Robert Artigiani, "The Name of the Wave: Science and Civilization in Prigogine and Eco," [Unpublished Paper], 15–16.
38. Braudel, *The Mediterranean*, Vol. I, 21.
39. *Ibid.*, Vol. II, 1244.
40. Artigiani, "The Name of the Wave," 17–18.
41. Braudel, *The Mediterranean*, Vol. I, 15–17.
42. *Ibid.*, Vol. II, 1238.
43. *Ibid.*, Vol. I, 17.
44. *Ibid.*, 902.
45. There are numerous other historians who could be discussed, in addition to Braudel, who have accepted this epistemology in part or in whole. They have not been discussed within the text because of limitations of space. An excellent analysis of the application of Prigogine to humanistic concerns is one by Robert Artigiani, who has demonstrated how Umberto Eco's *The Name of the Rose*, a study of medieval civilization, validates Prigogine. Other works of history which could be used to demonstrate the validity of Prigogine include: Colin Renfrew, *Antiquity and Men*, Cyril Stanley Smith, *A History of Metallography*, Jan Vansina, *Kingdoms of the Savanna*.
46. *The Social Sciences in Historical Study* [Bulletin 64], (New York: Social Science Research Council, 1954), 130, 136–137.
47. Winthrop Jordan, *White Over Black: American Attitudes Toward the Negro, 1550–1812* (N.Y.: Norton and Co., 1968), vii.
48. Jan Vansina, *Kingdoms of the Savanna* (Madison: University of Wisconsin Press, 1968).
49. Burke, ed., *A New Kind of History*, xii.
50. Hugh Trevor-Roper, *The Rise of Christian Europe* (N.Y.: Harcourt, Brace and World, 1965), 9.
51. Edward Hallet Carr, *What Is History?* (N.Y.: Alfred Knopf, 1972), 83.
52. Braudel, *The Mediterranean*, Vol. I, 21.

INDEX

95